HEARTBEAT FOR HORSES

Heartbeat for
HORSES

LAURA CHESTER & DONNA DEMARI

WILLOW CREEK PRESS

With special thanks to our superlative editor Andrea Donner,
and to the entire crew at Willow Creek Press, as well as to Ruth Naylor Miller.

Published by Willow Creek Press
P.O. Box 147, Minocqua, Wisconsin 54548

Editor: Andrea Donner

Library of Congress Cataloging-in-Publication Data:

Heartbeat for horses / edited by Laura Chester ; photographs by Donna Demari.
     p. cm.
  ISBN 1-59543-443-7 (hardcover : alk. paper)
 1. Horses–Literary collections. 2. Human-animal relationships–Literary collections.
I. Chester, Laura. II. DeMari, Donna
  PS509.H67H43 2007
  810.8'036296655–dc22
                        2006102221

Printed in Canada

With love for my mother
Marilyn DeMari

*

For my cousin, Helen Chester
In memory of our grandmother, Alice

CONTENTS

Introduction

Heartbeats

Hoofbeats

Drumbeats

MY LIFE WITH HORSES

Like many of you, I was a horse crazy girl. My first "true love" was Bunko. At fourteen hands, the top of his forelock and the top of my head were the exact same height. When I cut off a piece of his mane and tucked it into my own hair, you could not tell the difference. He had the mischievous habit of galloping along, putting his head down and stopping abruptly. Off I would roll over his neck occasionally landing on my feet. But then one sad winter Bunko got into the oat bin and foundered. I knew how he loved to eat, how the soft rattle of grain from across the field could make him shudder, how he'd ripple all over with the taste of it, stomping his hoof for *more, more*. It hurt me to hear the news, but I couldn't blame Bunko for over doing it.

I began to understand the power of words when my grandmother read me *Black Beauty*. She had to stop reading mid-chapter, moved by her own emotion. I was then inspired to start my own first fiction—*Betsy & Pixie Ride Again*, a story about a girl and her pony and their island adventures. Every time I completed a new section, I would bring the whole wad of paper downstairs and read the entire thing to my mother, whose only comment was, "I like it. It's getting better." How important that early encouragement was! As in the story, I too had to leave my idyllic country life and return to the city for school.

In town, I set up a sawhorse and rode right into the black and white television. My brother and I were wild about Westerns, until my mother decided we could not watch violence of any kind, and that included *Gunsmoke, Have Gun Will Travel, Wanted Dead or Alive*, and that meant we had to break the law.

At school we each created a scrapbook as a class project, anything of our choice, and of course my subject was *The History of Horses*, with information on just about everything. My friend Robin Grossman did her book on Russia. She even wrote Krushchev a letter, but she was bored by her subject while I never tired of mine. I could wile away an afternoon over a page of cowboy boots. For my efforts, I got an A, but my teacher didn't like Russia. She gave my friend a big C-. Robin cried, "But Krushchev never wrote back to me!"

I got the idea for a horse collection from my father who had collected china dogs when he was young. My own collection was an odd assortment, though of course I did have favorites, like the little white porcelain colt who bent down to scratch at his foreleg. Some were sets—a mare and a foal, or three porcelain palominos. There was also an agate burro and a racing horse made out of dark brown rubber. I called him something sleek, something dangerous—Cigarette. All of the horses had to have names. It was necessary to get a name that fit, like Frisky for the little bisque pony who trotted along so merrily.

The horses were entered by name in the horse shows I created on my bedroom floor. First the entries were all lined up (in stalls made out of pencils). Then they would be led out as events began. I timed each race and kept track of the winners. It must have looked a bit peculiar, with the big plastic horses running against the small china ones caught in a sleeping position, but I was the only witness. I used spools of thread for barrel racing, constructed miniature jumps and composed an intricate list in order to tabulate "Best in Show."

Since I'd never been introduced to the horse show circuit, I had to create my own venue. With banners on poles, homemade ribbons and trophies, I organized a rodeo out in the horse field. Everything went well until Betsy Sivage got up on Counterfeit and he started to buck. "Call the ambulance! Call the ambulance," she screamed until she fell. For all of my efforts, my grandfather gave me a tiny charm—a golden rider on a golden horse. I wore it around my neck for years and clutched it in my hand whenever my life seemed ready to run away with me.

I was only in two real horse shows—the first was a Walk-Trot-Canter class with five entries. I got a pink ribbon for fifth place. For some reason I was not at all ashamed and hung this emblem of dubious achievement up on my twin four poster. My second experience was in the Mississippi Rodeo, where I rode a friend's old white gelding, appropriately named Washtub. I was the only one riding bareback in the Musical Chair Contest. As soon as the music began to play, a light rain started to fall, but we kept galloping around and around until the needle was lifted— then we jumped from our mounts and raced through the muck, sliding to the closest chair available. Riding bareback gave me the extra advantage of getting off fast, but it also made it more difficult to tackle those sixteen hands of horse each time the music began. Finally, I tied with another fellow, and we had to flip a coin. He won. How I had wanted that ribbon!

The supreme highlight of my girlhood was becoming a Rough Rider at Teton Valley Ranch Camp out in Wyoming. We had a rodeo for five consecutive Sundays, and somehow I managed to accumulate the most points—pole bending, barrel racing, team roping, running our horses around the half-mile track. It was quite a triumph to beat the older Wranglers and Trail Blazers to win the coveted "Rodeo Queen" badge. I still remember the horse hair bracelets we made that summer, pulling course strands from the horses' manes, braiding black, white and brown all together, lighting the knot with a match, until it frizzled and sealed. The smell of burning hair always smelled like disaster. Even the stench of a blacksmith's hot shoe against a smoking hoof seemed alarming to me.

Because I grew up with a crew of twelve cousins, we all shared our horses. My grandmother, who was an avid rider, would often gift four of us (one leg each) with a new horse for Christmas. Since I was the oldest granddaughter, I often accompanied her on rides. With little warning she would take off. I learned to be ready, to enjoy the thrill of racing over the shorn fields, cantering through the woods.

At about this time, I favored Busytown, a huge brown hunter. My parents had just given me a ring, a thin band with a small heart on it. One day while riding Busy, he swerved and went straight for a maple, and I was struck, smacked out of the saddle. Gramma always said you weren't a real rider unless you had fallen off three times, but I'd already achieved that quota. Even though Busy had a canter like a rocker, even though he was a hunter and a jumper and a big prize winner, the ring on my finger was bent. My little gold heart was broke.

I only wished that I had been taught how to jump properly at an early age. I remember lying to my friend Lindsay Esser, saying that I could jump three feet. Though I was glad to have the burden of that lie lifted during my first confession, I still longed to fly like some of my equestrian friends who rode at The Milwaukee Hunt Club. But my riding life remained non-competitive. Most often I rode bareback with my cousin Helen. Together we rode through the rich melon smell of the mown fields, leaning forward to trace the delicate tip of an ear, or lying back on the horses' twin firm rumps, completely relaxed.

One August night, Helen and I snuck out from our sleeping porch beds to meet by the fence for a moonlight ride. She'd left two sets of reins on a gate post, and the horses, curious about our shapes in the dark, were easy to catch.

We loped through the fields, our pajama pants blowing. With moonlight tipped on the horse's manes and our blond hair, we were ghost riders, flashing primeval, almost weightless on our invisible saddles. It seemed mysteriously right to be riding, forbidden, and the horses too were casting their spells. The next morning, we found out that the horses had escaped. The gate was still locked. No fences down. They must have jumped, for a neighbor had seen them trotting freely down the road, corn silk hanging from their mouths. Helen and I were both quiet about it and didn't say a word, until years later I wrote her—"You know, it was after that night that we went riding bareback in the moonlight that I got my period for the first time." She replied, "And it was on that same night, I first felt my small breasts bounce and hurt."

When I went to Montana with my high school friend Nancy Puelicher, we stayed with her family at Elkhorn Ranch, and I got to ride a feisty quarter horse named Eagle. We rode deep into Yellowstone Park, where her father had to be air-lifted out by helicopter because of appendicitis. While Nancy swooned over Ringo and the Beatles, I fell in love with my chestnut, Eagle. He was a six year old cutting horse, full of power and energy. When I got back to Milwaukee, I was heart sick. I told my grandmother about him. She knew what it was like to be bonded to an animal, but still she asked, why *this* horse? "Because I love him," I said, and amazingly, my heart's wish was heard.

Months later, Gramma and I went down to the stockyard together. The place seemed relatively empty—only a few pigs were snorting around, some cows, but when I whistled and called his name, I finally saw his Eagle eyes shining through the slats. I climbed the ten foot rails into his pen. He looked good and hairy and awfully cute. The next day Gramma picked me up at school and off we went to the country. She let me drive even though I was under age. Eagle was in the pasture and he came right over though the other horses were being mean, ganging up on him. It hurt me to see how they picked on him, but soon he became their natural leader, and at last I had a horse of my own.

Eagle was hard to control. Even I had to saw him down sometimes or run him in a circle, but I was secure in the dark leather depth of his saddle. It had a well-worn golden pummel which melted when our barn burned to the ground. At least none of the horses were hurt. The new pole barn never had the soul of the old place, with its real hayloft and white-washed stalls. Its tiny tack room always smelled of well-oiled leather, while the new one had red carpet.

After summer was over, I rode Eagle in town. There's something romantic about riding all by yourself, with slicker strapped onto the back of your saddle, with sandwich and orange wrapped up inside. But that weekend, every motorcycle in the county seemed to race by me. I felt like I was riding home in the wrong century. Now motorcycles carried the outlaw. They polished chrome instead of leather. They didn't get to appreciate the joy of silence one got when riding alone.

Two years later I went away to college, and soon got married. Others now rode Eagle. He had mellowed with age. In fact, he was ridden right up to the end of his thirty-four years. I can still remember standing in the kitchen with a baby in my arms when I got the call from my father. Eagle had been put down. I could hardly believe it. Time stopped still. Time rewound—I was climbing the fence in the stockyard, sliding in the mud of the ring, knocked out of my saddle by a low hanging branch, tossed over the head of that mischievous pony, riding with both hands on the wooden cylinder that served as reins on my rocking horse, backward and forward at tremendous speed. Eagle, my horse, was gone. Dad said how all the other horses had come to the rail and whinnied after him when he was led down the dirt road. I cried out too, as if I were one of them. I felt that my girlhood was over.

But it is never over. It turns and returns in memory, even here on the page, in this collection of inspired writing, selections brought together in honor of all of you horse crazy girls, who can't get enough of the subject—who might only live in the fantasy world of books and statues, who dream of jumping like National Velvet, or who actually compete and win real ribbons, for the *escaramuza* girls who ride sidesaddle at a gallop, or for those who ride bareback out in the yard. May your dreams all come true. May you live life to the fullest as you find your way amongst these wonderful horses that have somehow, miraculously, come into your lives, big wonderful creatures who give us so much of their animal warmth, who bring us their stillness as well as their power, who give us the sound of their hoof beats, forever imprinting our hearts.

—Laura Chester, 2007

There in the distance, a noise I heard, it grew with every beat,
The tumbling, rumbling rhythm of two horses' flying feet.

But then their pace was gentled and round a twist they came,
A young girl and her grandmother rode by both mane to mane...

What better way to feel a part of all that's earth and sky
Than whirling over hill and dale on hoofs that seem to fly.

—Laura Chester, 1963

Heartbeats

White steed, white steed, most joy to thee,
Who still, with the first young glance of spring,
From under that glorious lake dost bring,
Proud steed, proud steed, my love to me.

—Thomas Moore

From: AUTOBIOGRAPHY OF A FACE

Lucy Grealy

The horses remained my one real source of relief. When I was in their presence, nothing else mattered. Animals were both the lives I took care of and the lives who took care of me. Horses neither disapproved nor approved of what I looked like. All that counted was how I treated them, how my actions weighted themselves in the world. I loved to stand next to them with no other humans in sight and to rest my head against their warm flanks, trace the whorls in their hide with the fingers of one hand while the other hand rested on the soft skin of their bellies. All the while, I'd listen to the patient sounds of their stomachs and smell the sweet air from their lungs as attentively as if I were being sent information from another world.

From: HORSE PEOPLE

Michael Korda

Margaret's desire to own a horse was clear enough early on in her life, by the age of four, when she came across two farm laborers having their lunch by the side of a lane while the horse that had been pulling their farm wagon, removed from the shafts, grazed nearby. It was a draft horse, a huge mare with feet as big as dinner plates, a massive neck, thick feathers around her fetlocks, and big square leather blinkers shading her eyes. Like most draft horses, she was friendly—sheer size seems to make such horses gentle—and more than willing to be patted by a little girl.

It didn't take long before Margaret's proprietary instincts were aroused, and she asked if she could take the mare home. The older of the two farm workers put down his bread and cheese and nodded— perhaps with a wink to his companion—then smiled. "If you can get 'er 'ome, you can 'ave 'er," he said, no doubt as a harmless piece of fun. In any case, Margaret took him at his word. So far as she was concerned, it was a bargain—the mare was as good as hers.

She took hold of the mare's bridle and pulled on it. The mare snorted, dropped her head, and continued to graze. Margaret pulled harder, tugging with all her might, but the harder she pulled, the more firmly the mare dug her feet in and stood rooted in place. She even tried to pick up each huge foot to get the mare moving, to no effect. Meanwhile, the two farm workers roared with laughter at the sight of a little girl, tears in her eyes, trying desperately to drag a horse that weighed close to a ton home with her. It's hard to know which was the most painful—the humiliation of being laughed at by a couple of loutish grown-ups, or the fact that the horse wouldn't budge for her.

Margaret pulled and pulled, but there was no moving the mare an inch. If there's one thing a big old draft horse knows, it's not to let itself be led away by a total stranger, however small and endearing—particularly when it's eating its lunch.

PRAISE BE

Maxine Kumin

Eleven months, two weeks in the womb
and this one sticks a foreleg out
frail as a dowel quivering
in the unfamiliar air and then
the other leg, cocked at the knee
at first, then straightening
and here's the head, a big blind fish
thrashing inside its see-through sack
and for a moment the panting mare
desists, lies still as death.

I tear the caul, look into eyes
as innocent, as skittery
as minnows. Three heaves, the shoulders pass.
The hips emerge. Fluid as snakes
the hind legs trail out glistening.
The whole astonished filly, still
attached, draws breath and whinnies
a treble tremolo that leaps
in her mother who nickers a low-key response.

Let them prosper, the dams and their sucklings.
Let nothing inhibit their heedless growing.
Let them raise up on sturdy pasterns
and trot out in light summer rain
onto the long lazy unfenced fields
of heaven.

From: SWEET WILLIAM

John Hawkes

The box stall was large, the sunlight came through an open window and lit the glistening straw and made it shine, as golden and translucent as the cicada's wings. A lark sang, Molly waited, paced slowly about the spacious stall, stood and waited. She raised her tail and held it there, a sure sign. She swung her head, looked behind her, patient but puzzled too, though over the years she had carried thirteen foals before me. Sam listened, gave her a nod, and then, precisely then, the waters broke, gushed forth; my hour was at last at hand. My dam, still standing, grunted as only the mare in labor can, and opened herself, and gently and firmly began to thrust me out. And the first human to touch me? Little Millie, who, with Jane's encouragement, seized my long thin protruding forelegs in her fists and pulled down, widened her eyes just as my newborn's head, about the size of that on the children's wooden rocking horse, came sliding into view along with my outstretched legs, head and face featureless, expressionless, slick and wet inside the tight membranes shrunken like a second translucent skin to my nose, my little jaw, my eyes, which were still sealed to the light and life of the world. Molly then lay down on her heavy side, gave another push, and now I was lying with my shoulders free, safe though not yet completely born, and Millie, young as she was, with her sweet fingers rent the membranes so as to free my nose, expose my nostrils to the breeze that now followed the shaft of warm sun into the stall. Sam nodded his old head, Molly whimpered in soft delight, and in another moment, another, out I slid as the Gordons laughed and nodded in approval, while the other mares and foals set up a distant welcoming clamor from atop the nearby hill, where they stood in the shade of the great oaks. My day, my hour, my introduction to serenity itself. And proud? Yes, Molly and the Gordons were all proud, but not half so proud as myself when my loving dam licked me and then prodded me to stand, tentatively, valiantly, with all my instincts already drawn to my mother's milk.

YEARLINGS IN THE PASTURE

Lyn Lifshin

no responsibility, just play
in the grass in a rose wind,
a butterfly wind. Before
harnesses, before shoes,

velvety bodies push and
shove, roll on their backs
squealing, chasing, becoming
the color of that rusty earth

THAT FIRST SUMMER

Lyn Lifshin

Ruffian ran free,
roamed meadow grass.
She nursed while
Shenanigans grazed.
As she grew bolder,
she explored the
paddock on her
own, nibbled at butter
flies, played with
stable hands, ran back
to her mother if
something startled
her. Birds, leaves, a
wind of clover
and roses. Then the
coolness of a maple
or oak when the
summer day
grew sweltering

From: BEAUTIFUL MY MANE IN THE WIND

Catherine Petroski

Just a little while ago, when I needed to go out to race a bit and throw my head in the wind, she stopped me and asked me who I thought I was. A girl? A horse? My name? I know what she's thinking. The others at school ask me the same question. So I said, A girl, because I know that's what I'm supposed to think. One thing I know, not a girlygirl, which would be stupid playing games talking teasing being tied to the jungle gym. I won't. Sometimes it's hard not telling her what I really think, what I know. That sometimes I'm a girl, sometimes I'm a horse. When there are girlthings to do, like read, which a horse never does, or go in the car to the stock show or for ice cream or any of those things, I have to be a girl, but when there are hillsides of grass and forests with lowhanging boughs and secret stables in loquat trees, I am a horse. Maybe someday there will be no changing back and forth and I will be stuck a horse. Which will be all right with me. Because horses think good easy things, smooth green and windy things, without large people or bothers or other kids or school, and they have enough grass to trot in forever and wind to throw their manes high to the sky and cool sweet stream water to drink, and clover.

From: KING OF THE WIND

Marguerite Henry

The boy Agba had not minded the fast for himself. It was part of his religion. But when Signor Achmet, Chief of the Grooms, commanded that the horses, too, observe the fast, Agba's dark eyes smouldered with anger.

"It is the order of the Sultan!" the Signor had announced to the horseboys. And he had cuffed Agba on the head when the boy showed his disapproval.

Of the twelve thousand horses in the Sultan's stables, Agba had charge of ten. He fed and watered them and polished their coats and cleaned their stalls. Best of all, he wheeled the whole string into the courtyard at one time for their exercise.

There was one of the ten horses to whom Agba had lost his heart. She was a bay mare, as fleet as a gazelle, with eyes that studied him in whatever he did. The other nine horses he would lead out to the common water trough to drink. But for his bright bay he would fill a water cask from a pure spring beyond the palace gates. Then he would hold it while the mare sucked the water, her eyelashes brushing his fingers as she drank. For long moments after she had drunk her fill, she would gaze at him while the cool water dribbled from her muzzle onto his hands.

From: HIDING GLORY

Laura Chester

As we rode, I could see dawn appearing in another world. The stars were like a sugar sprinkling behind us, glittering up the dark, while a whole new landscape was unfolding, with brilliant colors and vibrant bird songs. So, this was the country where children could play without mothers or teachers hanging over them.

When we landed, it was like bouncing on a great big cushion. I smelled something sweet, like apples or honey. The grass was so soft, it looked like feathers to me. Glory and I were both incredibly thirsty. I slid out of the saddle, and cupped my hands. It was the best tasting water I had ever had. It smelled of the forest, but it was sparkling clean. I wondered what we would eat when we got hungry.

"You've got strawberries hiding in your hair," Glory whispered, as if he could read my mind. I ran my fingers through my hair, and he was right. Delicious ripe berries fell into my hands. Deep in my pockets I found hard tack cookies. I nibbled on these and watched Glory graze on the soft green grass, until he had had his fill. "We're in Joya now," he proclaimed, "where your flowers and birds and mammals were named, before they were sent to earth."

I tried not to think about what would happen next, as Glory lay down beside me, resting his muzzle in my velvet lap. He wanted to nap before we continued. So, I let him sleep, stroking his forelock, gently unsnarling the tangles that had gathered in his mane. His muzzle was incredibly soft, and I stroked it too, and felt his grassy breath upon my leg. His nostrils quivered as he breathed in and out, and his eyelids seemed to flutter like petals.

I think I fell in love with Glory right there upon that mossy hillock, with Joya leaves wafting in the breeze overhead, sunlight filtering through them. He was as still and delicate as the most perfect flower. I felt like he was already my very best friend, and that we would always take care of each other.

From: THE ISLAND OF HORSES

Eilis Dillon

When we reached the grassy floor of the valley we went more slowly so as not to frighten the horses. As we approached them, they lifted their heads in that quick way that horses have. They looked at us steadily, but they did not run away. "They have never seen people before, I suppose," said Pat.

It was wonderful to walk up to them as they drank out of the stream or grazed peacefully and stroke their necks until their ears twitched with pleasure. Only the blacks were a little suspicious of us. The older ones sidled away and would not let us touch them. We let them alone, for we knew that if they fought us for possession of the colt, they would be sure to win the battle.

The colt was no more than seven or eight months old. His skin shone like the black satin bands on my mother's best skirt. His legs were so straight and slender that you wondered how they could hold him up at all, and his little round hooves shone like stones newly washed by the sea. He turned his long arched neck to look at us. There was such intelligence and understanding in his eyes that I said in a low voice:

"It's like taking a child from its mother, Pat."

"I can't go home without him," Pat repeated after a moment.

He put out his hand slowly and stroked the colt's neck. The colt shivered once and then moved closer to him. Very gently, we began to walk back to the strand, with the colt walking peacefully between us. He swished his long tail and seemed quite content. We kept our eyes on the other horses, but they took no notice of our departure. They had already gone back to their own pursuits.

Still, we were uneasy until we had rounded the end of the cliff and were crossing the silver strand. All the way back to the camp we kept looking fearfully behind us. We never stopped until we had the colt safely stabled in the hut. Then we blocked the door with furze bushes as best we could and sat down to eat our supper by the fire.

From: IN PRAISE OF HORSES

Mark Spragg

In the hot, late part of the summers we would often be camped in Eagle Creek meadows. Our camp was near the head of the long, tight valley, and the meadows spanned the half mile of the valley's bottom, the length of them stretching along the border of Eagle Creek for almost two miles. The mountains rose up abruptly in rock and timber on each side of the meadow, and down its center the creek wound and flattened, lost from view in the waist-deep grass. My brother and I would ride to the creek. We would strip off our clothes, saddles, boots, bridles, and remount cleanly, our naked heels against naked ribs, our buttocks clenched on the warm, haired spines of our horses, and ride stiffly into the water.

On the short, straight stretches the animals walked warily, as though on the skulls of mice we thought, belly-deep in the water, their hooves sucking at the graveled bottom. And in the bends, the water sluiced and deepened into a thick emerald green against green banks overhung with green grass, we would have to swim. We would grip the tufts of hair at the napes of their manes and rise toward the sun, slowly towed as the animals momentarily fell away from us, cooling in the water, lightly connected by our heat only. We would come out into the sun dripping, goose bumped, smiling wildly. We laughed. We hardly ever spoke. We lunged the horses into the water again.

A BRIEF SKETCH OF
MYSELF AT FOURTEEN

Lucy Grealy

Iwas riding Cocoa, and the last thing I remember is Lisa riding Eddie past me at a canter, something I'd specifically asked her not to do and for exactly this reason: The next thing I remember is Cocoa's hoof precisely in front of my face. I was on the ground, I knew that much; brown bubbles of water pressed out around Cocoa's thick, creased heel as her metal shoe sunk into the wet ground. I did not yet understand that my body was hanging, feet first, from the fence, and that only my head was on the ground. Turning my eyes and looking up, I followed the line of her leg from the heel up to her muddy elbows; I hadn't brushed her properly before saddling her. Her stomach, all wet from the puddles, was a revelation. I saw now how clearly round her underside was, how long, how elliptical, how perfect. The subtle, secret line of flesh drawn where one half of the body meets the other extended itself from her white, hairless belly button to the dark, soft mounds of her udder. The one back leg I could see was stretching and pointing up to the white, just-rained sky, like an arm pointing out an unusual plane or exotic bird passing by. All this quiet, even peaceful observation took place in a year's worth of seconds, in the few inches between myself and a broken skull. 'Hmmmm,' was all I could think to myself.

We all knew Cocoa bucked, and bucked like a pro when given even the slightest chance. I rode her anyway. She was 'my' horse, at least for a few weeks. Technically, of course, she belonged to Mr. Evans, who owned the hack barn I worked at along with half a dozen other kids, not for money but in exchange for free riding. Each of us, unable to afford our own horses and too ignorant to get real jobs at real stables, fell in love with different hack horses at Mr. Evans's barn by turn.

Ray, who'd worked there the longest, got to pick which horse was 'his' when a new selection arrived, then Lori did, then Lisa—who already 'had' Eddie—and so on down the hierarchical line. I was at the bottom. The horses left for me to pick, or which any of us picked really, in the end broke our hearts not through any of their numerous faults, but the world's, because we had to watch them be worked half to death, their mouths pulled and their sides kicked by huge city louts out for a day of fun in the faux country, a few acres of woods surrounded by housing developments. The flat-roofed, plywood barn was falling apart, and housewives from the surrounding neighborhoods were always calling the Department of Health to complain about the rats. There were a lot of rats. They scrambled for cover anytime you entered an aisle, and more than once I had to pull a drowned one out of a water bucket. Most of the horses didn't live in the barn, however, but in three small corrals surrounding the barn. Anything green had been eaten long ago, and when they weren't working, the hack horses just stood there. Summer and winter were okay, but in spring and fall the mud was so deep that the continuous, gritty moisture gave them something called 'scratches,' and the hair fell off their chapped ankles in infected, painful-looking scabs.

Like all the horses at the stable, Cocoa had come from the auction, a weekly Wednesday-night affair filled with dog-food dealers, alcoholic cowboys, and almost-bankrupt barn owners. It wasn't a place for million-dollar racehorses, or even decent horses someone might want to own privately. It was a place to unload problem horses, soured horses that bucked, kicked, or bit, and crippled horses, horses that would never be sound. Yet still, week after week after week, we begged Mr. Evans to let us go with him. We lived by tales of people who had good horses but were pressed for quick cash, and each week we kept waiting for such a bargain to be led into the small area in front of the auctioneer. And, of course, we always felt that even if we got a horse with a few problems, we could fix those problems, and we waited for those diamonds in the rough too, certain we'd be able to recognize them from across the dirt ring.

The auction ring and the makeshift stalls around it were set up under a huge array of outbuildings. In spring and fall the ground got so muddy wooden planks were laid lengthwise down the aisle so you could make your way through the puddles. In winter, this mud froze into a gray cast of footprints both horses and humans tripped over. In summer, it was all dust, and the water buckets held up with bailing twine were always empty.

None of this squalor mattered to me. I loved horses, and if this rough world was part of that love, then so be it. The auction was always crowded. All those human voices rising and converging in the air over our heads, punctuated by the loud shrill whinnies horses make when they're in a strange place. You had to be careful standing next to a horse's head at the auction, because he could let out a bursting whinny right next to your eardrum if you weren't observant enough to see it coming. Most of the horses there were destined for 'the meat man', the dog-food dealer, but it was something other than their physical worth to humans that thrilled me when they whinnied. Each horse had its own way of letting you know it was about to call out, but usually it was ears that pitched exactly forward, a tail lifted up, a neck just starting to arch, a horizontal line of muscles just starting to show on their sides as they took a deep breath. When I saw those moves I took half a step back and watched the horse whinny, its eyes large, its mouth half open, its nostrils so wide you could see the deep purple inside. Something which had nothing to do with any of us humans, or with the various shapes of human sadness we forced those bedraggled, doomed horses to inhabit, shone at that moment.

Cocoa was so named because of her chocolate-colored coat. I rode her even though she bucked because, not yet burdened by any actual knowledge of the details of horse training, I imagined she bucked because she was unhappy. I would make her happy, and because I thought that to be happy must equal being loved, I would let her know I loved her. It seemed so simple. I brought her carrots, I brushed her, I put my small, thin arms around her neck. I confided in her, told her that I understood what it was to be unhappy, confessed that I would probably have bucked too.

It is always men who want to push forward certain theories about why adolescent girls love horses so much, want to explain it in terms of sex, or the desire to be near such power. What do they know? What do they know, with their early childhood fixations, with their small hard bodies that point them so easily and so early toward what they think they want? What do they know of sensuousness unbound by form, of desire so unfocused it doesn't yet have a name, and doesn't even want one, desire fulfilled only by the very act of desiring itself? I *loved* those horses.

Cocoa never stopped bucking. Mr. Evans, fearing a lawsuit, put her back in the trailer a few Wednesdays later. I wasn't there when they took her away. I turned my attentions toward the next candidate: Boone, a mild-mannered Appaloosa I came to love more than life itself. Boone stayed at the stable for years, allowing me to love him, but I also understood he'd never amount to all that much in the equine world. Then, every once in awhile, a horse like Cocoa came along, a quality horse except for the fact there was something invisibly 'wrong' with her; spoiled goods. Horses like Cocoa broke my heart, not because of the thing 'wrong' with them, but because, despite every dedicated ounce in my body, I could not fix that wrong thing. I could not do it.

And though any place was better than being at home, the stable was not an easy place to spend time; my fingers swelled and turned so useless in the winter I couldn't undress myself afterward in the garage, where my mother made me go because I was so dirty. In the summer the hay stuck like needles to my drenched shirt, sticking me whenever I lifted my arms over my head or tried to lean back in a moment of rest. When I undressed at night, bits of chaff fell from my clothes like confetti. I was working the work of a grown man for no pay, was bullied by the older kids for my assorted physical and emotional shames, and my romantic heart cringed at the sight of each broken-down horse, but still, I did not know how to find, or even name, any other place to be.

Without understanding it, we were mistreating those horses. We didn't know it was wrong to feed horses cattle feed, which we did when short of cash because it was cheaper. We didn't understand why the hay

was always moldy and yellow, despite the obvious fact we bought only the cheapest and stored it improperly. A vet only rarely stepped foot on the place, and only then because a horse was near death. We didn't have the money for everyday vet calls, so instead we were always treating raging infections with bottles of hydrogen peroxide, stitching up wounds with sewing needles and without local anesthetic while someone else 'twitched' the horse to keep it still, which involved wrapping a chain tightly around the soft tissue of the horse's upper lip. They'd twist their head and roll their eyes back and freeze into a trembling standstill, more afraid of the pain from the twitch than anything else we could do to them.

My adult self looks back on all this and sees something avoidably sad. My adult self sees how I willed myself to stay there despite the unhappiness, because as a child, and for too long as an adult, I could only gauge how much I loved something by how much it hurt me. My adult self looks back on these days and thinks, What a shame; it didn't have to be this way.

What does she know? What does she know with her theories of co-dependence, of mental health, of how it 'should be'? What does she know with her adult forgetfulness of what children know about loneliness and love, about how we are *always* trying our best, despite what the adults tell us? Those horses were muddy and skinny and filled with worms, but when I ran my hands down the articulated bones of their legs, or rested my head against their barrel-chested sides, the secret luminous truth of how wretchedness and joy are inseparable brushed past me, and sometimes it was almost as if I'd heard its rustle; so many times—myself alone in the dirty tack room, or at night turning out all the lights and locking up, or walking across a field to find a thrown shoe—my young self suddenly stopping and turning her head, listening for something she hadn't quite heard, something already gone, if it had been there at all. I *loved* those horses.

The people who came out from the city to rent horses rarely got their money's worth. Though some horses, like Boone, were well-behaved, their goodness only made it harder for them: Hackers ran them into the ground. The hackers brought the horses back heaving, covered with sweat, foam dripping down from under the saddle, and would tell us what a great time they had. Since Boone was 'my' horse, almost weekly I had to watch this happen, had to go hide in the tack room and wait out my sadness.

But not all the horses were so naïve. The stables were at the bottom of a gently sloping hill, and the trail wound its way up around this hill. For the first quarter mile the hackers and their horses were in plain view and the horses, however grudgingly, plodded forward. But then the trail turned and became obscured by trees, and the horses understood the exact spot at which they could stop in their tracks and start eating leaves. Most people who came to our stable didn't have a clue about riding and all their yanking and kicking meant nothing to the horse. Soon they'd start calling for help. Secretly proud of the horses, we'd ignore the hackers' cries for help unless Mr. Evans was around, in which case we'd take turns going up and 'rescuing' the riders. At least a few times on a busy day, people complained.

'These horses don't go!' they'd shout at Mr. Evans.

'You just can't ride, that's the problem.'

'I can too ride. I took lessons at camp. These horses suck. They won't move.'

At this point, Mr. Evans would turn and hope I was around, because I was particularly effective for this specific stunt.

'I bet that skinny little girl could make that horse go.'

'I want my money back!' the hackers complained, as if money could solve all this, allow them to wash their hands of this dissolution and walk away clean.

'If that skinny girl can't get this horse to go, I'll give you your money back.'

It's true, I was very skinny, and underdeveloped; I looked utterly powerless. Most of the time, my body was an embarrassment.

I stepped up to hold the horse while its rider clumsily climbed down, grunting and often almost pulling the saddle off with them.

The horse knew the routine, and as I stepped up to him to take the reins, he'd eye me sideways and try to step away as the disgruntled hacker crossed his arms and watched.

Knowing exactly who I was, the newly rehabilitated horse began hopping in nervous circles while I put one foot in the stirrup. Mr. Evans had to hold the bridle because otherwise the horse would take off at a full gallop during that vulnerable second after I'd jumped up but before I'd actually landed in the saddle. I wondered how the customers could not have caught on. Once up in the saddle, and without bothering to put my feet in the stirrups, all I had to do was point the animal beneath me in the right direction and off we'd go with a clattering of hooves, leaving everyone behind to stand on the rocky ground, the quick four-beat gait smooth as anything, the wind pressing my shirt against my body. I liked to glance down and see the hard, packed dirt of the trail slip beneath us, the galloping horse's leg reaching out as if to grab that ground and pull it toward us while the leaves of a few low branches touched the top of my hair.

This was the moment I dreamed of, always, before I had ever been on a horse, before I knew I wanted this moment but wanted it nonetheless, and it was this moment I would keep dreaming of all my adult life. Galloping up and away in a smooth commotion of silent, eternal thrill, the simultaneous flying embrace both from and of the world. It was this moment exactly, except, as I reached the top of the hill where I'd maybe spin the horse around a couple of times for effect, I began to remember that this moment was surrounded by other moments. I still wanted this moment of galloping exactly, but as I turned back toward the stable, I also knew that I wanted it someplace else, under different circumstances; this moment exactly, but in a different moment. If I had my own horse, if I could become rich and rescue Boone from this grassless place, or if I could become smart enough and good enough to rescue a horse like Cocoa, if I could transform her into something 'right', or if for some sudden and miraculous reason whatever horse I *was* on could suddenly *want* to be stretching forward like this, out into what seemed like an endless chance, *then* I could live in this syncopated, enraptured moment forever, with desire being nothing more complicated than the pure, honorable link between me and the rest of the world.

For now, for effect, I held the reins lightly, and the small crowd I was galloping toward would begin to step back in alarm just as I pulled up short in a breath of dust. Dropping the reins across the horse's neck, I'd nonchalantly throw my leg over the saddle and jump the long distance down, landing with a thud to make sure everyone watching understood that I did not give a shit about a single thing in this world.

'See,' Mr. Evans would say, turning to the silenced, still irate customer.

SHE HOLDS HER FAVORITE COWBOY CLOSE

Paul Zarzyski

Wristwatch strapped over his cuff, a hand
thick as a tractor manifold
pivots off his daughter's shoulder, his arm
looped around her with savvy
he's used to slip bridles
on 45 years of colts—*easy now*—
as not to spook a single curl
tumbling beneath the powder-blue Resistol—
easy now—as not to foul with diesel or grease,
or the smell of hooves he's just shod,
her cotton boot-length dress, her satin sash
embossed in silver. She's the crowned
queen and sweetheart of the Fremont County Fair
& Rodeo. No mimicked cowboy myth
poses against *their* yard fence—
the burrowings of bark beetles in slab
pickets like swivel-cut leather—
against spirited horses grazing
blurred acres beyond the camera's depth of field.
No fat or phony frills taint *this* span
of father-daughter, lean grin and wide smile
matching perfectly the casts
of their trophy buckles beaming side by side,
and the speckle-faced Aussie cowdog, squatting
perk-eared and cocked for some action he craves
outside this frame. The West before wire
still rides the lineage of this family ranch
where broncs, pastured with the bridlewise,
fashion a soft backdrop for lovers
of horses—like father, like daughter—
blue-ribboned in their Wind River embrace

From: MISTY OF CHINCOTEAGUE

Marguerite Henry

Quickly Paul scrambled over the fence. He waited again, his eyes fastened on the spot where the Pied Piper's band stood huddled. He held onto the fence with one hand and made a watershed over his eyes with the other. He waited again for the lightning. It came tearing across the sky. He could see the Pied Piper's family as plainly as if it were daylight, but the Phantom and Misty were not among them. They were gone! Stolen! Some other stallion had stolen them! The thought flashed through his mind.

Shivering and drenched, he ran from one band to the other. He stumbled over tree stumps and fell flat in the water. His mouth was gritty with sand and mud. He went on blindly, feeling every hump in the grass, every fallen log; but nowhere in all that big corral could he find the tiny foal or her wild dam.

Running, slipping, falling, running, he made his way to the pony trucks. Most of the trucks were empty, waiting for tomorrow's sale. A few held a colt or two—big colts, big and shaggy.

Sick with fear for Phantom and Misty, he sought the shelter of Grandpa Beebe's truck to think out where they might be. Could Phantom have leaped the fence? Could Misty have rolled out under it? He stopped short. There, in the body of the truck, under a piece of tarpaulin, he felt rather than saw a slight stirring. He trembled, not from cold, but from fear that what he prayed was a mare and her colt would turn out instead to be bags of feed. He cried out for a flash of lightning. It came in a streak, filling the truck with yellow light. And in that split second Paul saw the Phantom and Misty, their heads lowered in a corner like children being punished at school.

He threw back his head for joy and let the rain beat on his face. So that was why Grandpa's shirt was torn and his face seamed with dirt! He had brought them to shelter before the storm broke.

Paul opened the door of the cab, half expecting Grandpa to be there. It was empty—except for Grandpa's old rain jacket that lay on the seat, and the strong smell of tobacco. He ripped off his wet shirt, his denim pants. His teeth chattered as he pulled on the warm, dry jacket. It was so long it almost covered his underwear. He ran around to the tailgate of the truck and steadied himself on the spare tire. Slowly, cautiously, hardly daring to breathe, he climbed up and over the tailgate and into the truck.

The storm blotted out any sound he might have made. But the Phantom sensed his presence. She neighed sharply to Misty, who caught her fear. Paul could hear the small rat-a-tat of her hooves.

He leaned hard against the stakes of the truck, every muscle tensed. Phantom would either charge him or stay as far away as possible. He waited, counting the seconds. He could hear the rain sloshing over the tarpaulin, spilling down the sides of the truck. He could smell the steamy warmth of furry bodies. He could smell the sea. And in the occasional flashes of light, he saw the copper-and-white tail of the Phantom sweeping nervously over Misty. Paul let out a deep sigh of relief. She was *not* going to charge him.

He never knew how long he stood there. He only knew that after awhile the Phantom no longer mistrusted him. She seemed to doze off for seconds at a time, as if she felt a oneness with him; as if she and her foal and this shivering, wet boy were fellow creatures caught in a storm, prisoners of the elements. Prisoners together.

Together! The word sounded a bugle in Paul. Time stood still. There was only the wind and the rain and the three creatures together! Together!

Aching to reach out and touch first the shaggy coat, then the silky one, he plunged his hands deep into Grandpa's pockets to stay the impulse. His fingers felt a firm, slightly sticky object. He squeezed it. He traced a few dried stems, then paper-thin leaves pressed solidly together. It was a twist of chewing tobacco! Quickly he pulled it out of his pocket. The spicy sweetness of molasses filled his nostrils. He took long, deep breaths of it. His mind was turning somersaults. Molasses! Molasses! How ponies love it! Often he had seen Grandpa cut a quid for Watch Eyes. With trembling fingers he broke off a sizeable piece and held it on his outstretched hand.

For a long time he waited. When he could stand no longer, he sank down on the cold, wet floor of the truck, still holding his hand toward the Phantom.

He waited, motionless.

He listened to the storm bell tolling out in the bay, and to the rain swishing and swirling around him. He felt little rivulets of perspiration run down his back. He grew hot and chilled by turns. His arm grew numb, then began to prickle as if hundreds of red-hot needles were jabbing him. His head reeled. It ached for lack of sleep.

And just when his hand was about to drop, he heard slow, questioning hooves placed one at a time on the floor of the truck. One step forward. Then a long pause filled in by the sobbing of the wind. Then another step. And another. Now a breath on his hand, now feelers sending chills of excitement up his arm, racing through his whole body. Now a soft muzzle lipping his palm. The tobacco gone! Lifted out of his hand by a pony so wild that she had upset a boat, so wild that for two years no one had caught her. A wild thing eating out of his hand! He wriggled his fingers in wonderment. All the numbness had gone out of them. He was not even trembling! Only this sharp ecstasy, this feeling that all of life was worth this moment. The roundup, the discovery of Misty, the swim across the channel—they all melted into this.

The moments rushed on. The storm quieted. Paul could hear the Phantom mouthing the tobacco. He tried to keep awake to enjoy the pleasant, soothing sound, but his eyes drooped. His breath steadied. He fell into a deep sleep, unmindful when the Phantom nosed him curiously from head to foot. Then she, too, began to doze.

At last Misty sank down in exhaustion. Her head fell across Paul's lap, not because she wanted human comfort, but because she was tired from the hard drive and the swim. The floor of a truck or a boy's lap were all the same to her, so long as her dam was near.

It was thus, at dawn, that Grandpa Beebe found them.

From: THE GHOST HORSE
Chief Buffalo Child Long Lance

One of our subchiefs, Chief Mountain Elk, now went through our camp, quietly giving instructions for all hands to line themselves along the great runway to "beat in" the herd. Every woman, old person, and child in the camp was called up to take part in this particular phase of the drive. We children and the women crept over to the runway and sprawled ourselves along the outside of the fence, while the men went beyond the fenced part of the runway and concealed themselves behind the brush and logs—where it was a little more dangerous.

Thus we crouched on the ground and shivered quietly for an hour or more before we heard a distant "Ho-h!... Ho-h!" It was the muffled driving cry of our warriors, the cry which for ten days they had been uttering to the horses to let them know that no harm could come to them from this sound. Thus, the horses did not stampede, as they would have done had they not recognized this noise in the darkness.

We youngsters lay breathless in expectancy. We had all picked out our favorite mounts in this beautiful herd of wild animals; and to us as we lay there, it was like the white boy lying in bed waiting for Santa Claus. Our fathers had all promised us that we could have the ponies that we had picked, and we could hardly wait to get our hands on them. My favorite was a beautiful calico pony, a roan, white, and red pinto—three different colors splashed on his shoulders and flanks like a crazy-quilt of exquisite design. He had a red star on his forehead between his eyes, and I had already named him Naytukskie-Kukatos, which in Blackfoot means One Star.

Presently we heard the distant rumble of horses, hooves—a dull booming which shook the ground on which we lay. Then, "Yip-yip-yip, he-heeh-h-h," came the night call of the wolf from many different directions. It was our braves signaling to one another to keep the herd on the right path. From out of this medley of odd sounds, we could hear the mares going, "Wheeeeeh-hagh-hagh-hagh"—calling their little long-legged sons to their sides that they might not become lost in the darkness and confusion.

Our boyish hearts began to beat fast when we heard the first loud "Yah! Yah! Yah!" We knew that the herd had now entered the brush portion of the runway, and that our warriors were jumping up from their hiding places and showing themselves with fierce noises, in order to stampede the horses and send them racing headlong into our trap.

Immediately there was a loud thunder of pattering hooves. Horses crying and yelling everywhere, like convulsive human beings in monster confusion. Above this din of bellowing throats and hammering feet, we heard one loud, full, deep-chested roar which we all recognized, and it gave us boys a slight thrill of fear. It sounded like a cross between the roar of a lion and the bellow of an infuriated bull. It was the massive steel-dust stallion, furious king of the herd. In our imagination we could see his long silver tail thrown over his back, his legs lashing wide apart, and stark murder glistening from the whites of those terrible eyes. We wondered what he would do to us if he should call our bluff and crash through that fence into our midst.

From: NATIONAL VELVET

Enid Bagnold

In Tablet Gully the piebald cropped, moving from tuft to tuft in sun and shadow, and flashing as he moved. The bone of his shoulder, thrown up by his stooping neck, rippled under his sliding skin. His parti-colored mane hung forward over his neck, and his long tail tipped the ground.

He swung round with the sun. His teeth tore evenly as he worked. Now his quarters could be seen, slightly pearshaped and faulty, but strong. His hocks, too thick, but straight and clean, waded in the burnt grasses. He lifted a sloping pastern finished with a pink hoof, and bit a fly off his leg. The clouds reared overhead, the legendary gully with its dead man's tablet was heavy with steady sun and shielded from the wind.

Among the scabious flowers on the north slope sat Velvet, steady as a gorse bush, cross-legged, and watching the horse. She had tied Sir Pericles to a gate in the valley behind her.

Sitting like a Buddha, dreaming of the horse, riding the horse in her dreams. A piece of cake and a Mar's Bar beside her in a paper bag, and the insects hummed and the mauve August flowers hardly moved. Just to look at him her heart beat violently with ambition. Her strong and inexperienced imagination saw no barriers. She was capable of apprehending death and of conceiving fame—in her own way, not for herself but for her horse. For a shilling she had won this wild creature that did not know its strength. In this valley, tucked away, she had got glory. What she meant to do made her heart beat afresh. She looked steadily at the piebald as though she pitied him. Eating his grass, prince, with his kingdom waiting for him! Her hand stole out and pulled the Mar's Bar from its bag, and she sucked its heavy stump, made from milk chocolate, toffee and nuts.

All the Hullocks were creeping with dowdy animals at livery. But here in Tablet Gully moved on its clever legs this living horse. Pulling gently at a blister on her heel she rode him in her mind. She would dazzle the world with this spot of luck, she and the creature together, breathing like one body, trying even to death, till their hearts burst. She would place her horse where he belonged, in history. She clasped the Mar's Bar like a prophet's child, with both hands.

Hoofbeats

The hoofs of the horses!—Oh! Witching and swee[t]
Is the music earth steals from the iron-shod feet;
No whisper of lover, no trilling of bird,
Can stir me as hoofs of the horses have stirred.

—Will H. Ogilvie

From: THE JOY OF MAN'S DESIRING
Jean Giono

But, above all, there was that drumming of the blood, the rumbling of the blood. It thumped in both men and women upon a deep-sounding drum. At each blow, it struck as it were the hollow of the breast. Each felt bound to this cadence. It was like the blades of a threshing machine. It was like the flail that strikes the grain, flies back, strikes the grain, flies back. It was like the travail of the man leaping in the wine vat. It was like the steady gallop of a horse. If he gallops like that, constantly, with his heavy hoofs, he will go to the end of the world, and beyond the end of the world he will gallop through the sky, and the vault of the heavens will resound at his passage as the earth is resounding now. Always, always, without ceasing, because blood does not cease to beat, to explore, to gallop, and to demand with its black drum to join the dance.

From: THE ISLAND OF HORSES

Eilis Dillon

It was pitch dark when I awoke. The star was gone. I lay very still, hoping that sleep would steal over me again. Then I began to notice what I suppose must have disturbed me. The ground under me seemed to be shaking gently. I listened with every part of me. My very hair seemed to go rigid with a terrible, primitive fear. Over and over my mind kept repeating the words: *The Island of Horses, the Island of Horses*. The shaking of the earth became a sound. There was no mistaking it. It was the sound of hoof beats on turf. With a cry of fear, I seized Pat's arm and pushed him, rattled him about until he started awake. His voice was easy and sensible.

"Danny, what is it? Don't be afraid."

"Don't you hear it? It's horses, horses galloping."

He reached out for my shoulder and held it so that I stopped trembling, while he listened. Then he said softly:

"Yes, horses galloping."

I felt him twitch the blanket aside. We got up. Still holding my shoulder, he moved toward the doorway. I went with him in a half-dream. The noise was deafening now. Ever so still we stood, hardly breathing, looking out over our barricade of furze. The sky was dark and there was no moon, but a faint grayness might have been the beginning of the dawn. Then past the hut came the horses, thundering along the grassy track. We saw nothing but a mass of flying shadows. Down past the quay they went, and along the island to the south, where we had not yet been. We listened until the sound of their hooves died away. Long after that, we were still listening, thinking that the beating of our own hearts was the drumming of hooves.

From: THE GOOD MASTER

Kate Seredy

When they reached the wagon, there was more trouble. Kate declared that since the wagon had no top, she'd get a sunstroke. It didn't have cushions on the seat, so she'd break to pieces. She told Father to "phone" for a "taxicab."

"I'll wash you mouth out with soap, if you swear at *my* father!" cried Jancsi. "Phone" and "taxicab" sounded like swearing to him.

"She wasn't swearing, Jancsi," said Father; "she is just talking city language. 'Phone' is a little black box, you can talk into it, and people many miles away hear you. 'Taxicab' is a horseless wagon city people travel in." He turned to Kate. "We haven't any taxicabs here, Kate, so come on, hop on the seat."

Kate shook her head. "I will not. Ride in this old wagon indeed! Why, everybody will laugh at me."

Father's patience was wearing out. He just grabbed Kate under the arms and lifted her into the seat before she knew what had happened. "Come on, Son, we can't waste the whole day. You sit on the outside so she won't fall off." They both got on the wagon. Kate almost disappeared between them. Father was a very big man, and Jancsi a big husky boy for his age. But what Kate lacked in size, she made up in temper. When she realized what had happened, she turned into a miniature whirlwind. She kicked and screamed, she pinched Jancsi, she squirmed like a "bag of screaming monkeys."

"Father, the man was right, she's a bag of screaming monkeys!" said Jancsi, half angry, half amused, holding on to Kate.

Father was busy holding the horses in check. They were respectable farm horses, not used to the unpleasant sounds Kate managed to make. Soon they left the town and were traveling at a fast clip on the country road. Little by little Kate subsided. The long trip in the train and all the excitement were beginning to wear her out. She looked around. She saw the great Hungarian plain unfold before her eyes. Something in her was touched by the solemn beauty of it. Its immense

grassy expanses unbroken by mountains or trees, shimmering under the spring sun. The dark blue sky, cloudless, like an inverted blue bowl. Herds of grazing sheep, like patches of snow. No sound, save the soft thud of the horses' hoofs on the white dusty road, and now and then the distant tinkle of sheep's bells, or the eerie sound of a shepherd's flute, the tilinkó. At times these plains, called the "puszta," are the very essence of timeless calm. At times the puszta wakes up and resembles an ocean in a storm. Clouds, so low it seems you can reach up and touch them, gather above. Hot winds roar over the waving grass. Frightened herds stampede, bellowing and crying. But calm or stormy, it is magnificent. Its people are truly children of the soil, they are like the puszta itself. Good-natured, calm, smiling, they, like the plain, can be aroused to violent emotions.

Kate did not know all this, but she was touched by the greatness and calm of it. She was very quiet now. Jancsi looked at her and touched Father's shoulder. They smiled at each other—she seemed asleep. Jancsi felt almost sorry for her now, she was so little and thin, so funny with her dirty little face. "Like a kitten," he thought, "the poor little kitten I found after the storm." He moved, to give her more room. She leaned heavily against him, her head nodding. He didn't see her face now, didn't see the slow impish grin, the awakening mischief in her eyes. He moved a little more, balancing on the edge of the seat. "Poor little kitten," he thought again—and "poor little kitten" suddenly gave him a hearty push which sent him off the wagon like a bag of flour. He landed in the dusty road, resembling a bag of flour indeed. He hurt something awful where he landed; it was the same spot Máli the cow had kicked that morning. Through the dust he saw the wagon come to a stop.

Father jumped down and, reaching Jancsi, began to feel his arms and legs for broken bones. "You great big baby," he scolded, "you want to ride wild horses? Can't even stay on a wagon!"

"Hey! Hey! Father! Stop Kate! Look, Father!" Jancsi yelled, struggling away from Father.

There was Kate, standing bolt upright on the seat, reins and whip in hand. She was grinning from ear to ear.

"Pushed you off, didn't I, little girl? Catch me if you can!" She whipped the horses, screaming at them: "Gee, git up, git up!" This was too much for one day even for the horses. They lunged forward, and broke into a wild gallop.

Father, shocked speechless for a moment, grabbed Jancsi by the arm.

"Come on, Son, we've got to catch this screaming monkey before the horses break their legs, or she breaks her neck!"

They ran, panting and choking in the hot dust. The wagon was almost out of sight now.

"Got-to-get-horses!" panted Father.

"We-could-catch-two from the herd here!" choked Jancsi, pointing to the herd they had passed that morning.

They jumped the fence and were among the surprised horses before the animals became alarmed.

"Run with the horse, Son," cried Father. "Run with it, grab its mane, and *swing*!"

Exciting moments followed. They were used to horses, but this was hard business, without rope or halter. Jancsi singled out a young chestnut horse. The animal reared, shied, baring his teeth, and started to run. But Jancsi's hands were already clutching his mane. The horse broke into a wild run, Jancsi clinging to him for dear life. He was carried like a piece of cloth, almost flying beside the horse. With a supreme effort he pulled himself up. Clutching his legs around the animal's neck, he reached forward to pull its nose down. Horse and rider were a mass of plunging, snorting animation. Jancsi was dizzy, but he gritted his teeth and hung on. Then he heard Father's voice through the tumult. "Let him run and guide with your knees. Come on 'csikós,' you're a real son of mine!"

Slowly the horse quieted down. Jancsi pulled him around and headed for the fence. Father was riding a big mare, waving to him to follow. Soon they were traveling side by side—hot, dirty, exhausted, and, judging by Father's face, madder than hornets.

They rode through the village without stopping to ask questions. The poplars on the ranch road whizzed past them. There was the house now! There was Mother, at the gate, waving madly with one hand. With her other hand she was clutching the blue skirts of a dancing, struggling little imp—a dirty, disheveled, but grinning little girl—cousin Kate from Budapest!

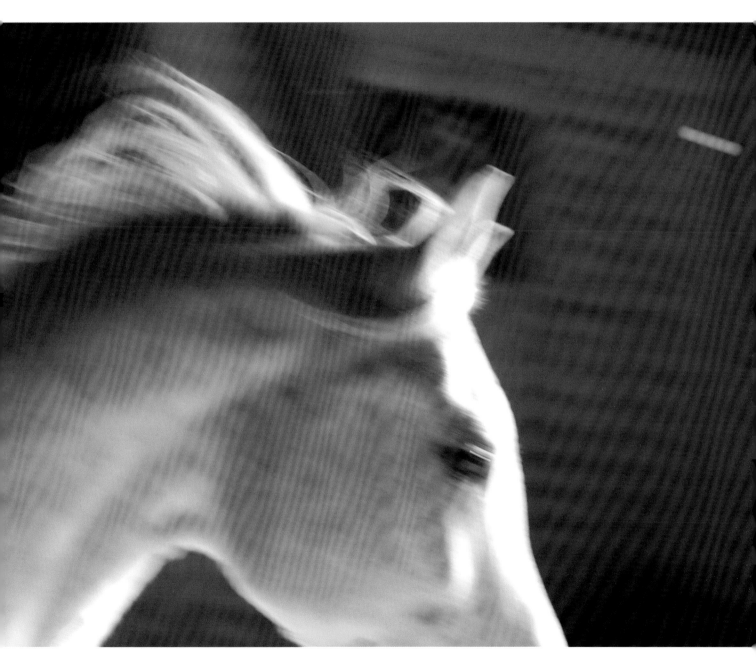

From: CHU CHU

Bret Harte

With an air of demure abstraction she permitted me to mount
her, and even for a hundred yards or so indulged in a mincing
maidenly amble that was not without a touch of coquetry. Encouraged
by this, I addressed a few terms of endearment to her, and in the exu-
berance of my youthful enthusiasm I even confided to her my love for
Consuelo, and begged her to be "good" and not disgrace herself and
me before my Dulcinea. In my foolish trustfulness I was rash enough
to add a caress, and to pat her soft neck. She stopped instantly with an
hysteric shudder. I knew what was passing through her mind: she had
suddenly become aware of my baleful existence.

The saddle and bridle Chu Chu was becoming accustomed to, but
who was this living, breathing object that had actually touched her?
Presently her oblique vision was attracted by the fluttering movement
of a fallen oak leaf in the road before her. She had probably seen many
oak leaves many times before; her ancestors had no doubt been famil-
iar with them on the trackless hills and in field and paddock, but this
did not alter her profound conviction that I and the leaf were identi-
cal, that our baleful touch was something indissolubly connected. She
reared before that innocent leaf, she revolved round it, and then fled
from it at the top of her speed.

The lane passed before the rear wall of Saltello's garden.
Unfortunately, at the angle of the fence stood a beautiful madroño
tree, brilliant with its scarlet berries, and endeared to me as Consuelo's
favorite haunt, under whose protecting shade I had more than once
avowed my youthful passion. By the irony of fate Chu Chu caught
sight of it, and with a succession of spirited bounds instantly made for
it. In another moment I was beneath it, and Chu Chu shot like a
rocket into the air. I had barely time to withdraw my feet from the stirrups, to throw up one arm to protect my glazed sombrero and grasp
an overhanging branch with the other, before Chu Chu darted off. But
to my consternation, as I gained a secure perch on the tree, and looked

about me, I saw her—instead of running away—quietly trot through the open gate into Saltello's garden.

Need I say that it was to the beneficent Enriquez that I again owned my salvation? Scarely a moment elapsed before his bland voice rose in a concentrated whisper from the corner of the garden below me. He had divined the dreadful truth!

"For the love of God, collect to yourself many kinds of thees berry! All you can! Your full arms round! Rest tranquil. Leave to your ole oncle to make for you a delicate exposure. At the instant!"

He was gone again. I gathered, wonderingly, a few of the larger clusters of parti-colored fruit, and patiently waited. Presently he reappeared, and with him the lovely Consuelo—her dear eyes filled with an adorable anxiety.

"Yes," continued Enriquez to his sister, with a confidential lowering of tone but great distinctness of utterance, "it is ever so with the American! He will ever make *first* the salutation of the flower or the fruit, picked to himself by his own hand, to the lady where he call. It is the custom of the American hidalgo! My God—what will you? I make it not—it is so! Without doubt he is in this instant doing thees thing. That is why he have let go his horse to precede him here; it is always the etiquette to offer these things on the feet. Ah! behold! it is he!—Don Francisco! Even now he will descend from thees tree! Ah! You make the blush, little sister (archly)! I will retire! I am discreet; two is not company for the one! I make tracks! I am gone!"

How far Consuelo entirely believed and trusted her ingenious brother I do not know, nor even then cared to inquire. For there was a pretty mantling of her olive cheek, as I came forward with my offering, and a certain significant shyness in her manner that were enough to throw me into a state of hopeless imbecility. And I was always miserably conscious that Consuelo possessed an exalted sentimentality, and a predilection for the highest medieval romance, in which I knew I was lamentably deficient. Even in our most confidential moments I was always aware that I weakly lagged behind this daughter of a gloomily distinguished ancestry, in her frequent incursions into a vague but poetic past. There was something of the dignity of the Spanish châtelaine in the sweetly grave little figure that advanced to accept my specious offering. I think I should have fallen on my knees to present it, but for the presence of the all-seeing Enriquez. But why did I even at that moment remember that he had early bestowed upon her the nickname of "Pomposa"? This, as Enriquez himself might have observed, was "sad and strange."

I managed to stammer out something about the madroño berries being at her "disposicion" (the tree was in her own garden!), and she took the branches in her little brown hand with a soft response to my unutterable glances.

But here Chu Chu, momentarily forgotten, executed a happy diversion. To our astonishment she gravely walked up to Consuelo and, stretching out her long slim neck, not only sniffed curiously at the berries, but even protruded a black underlip towards the young girl herself. In another instant Consuelo's dignity melted. Throwing her arms around Chu Chu's neck she embraced and kissed her. Young as I was, I understood the divine significance of a girl's vicarious effusiveness at such a moment, and felt delighted. But I was the more astonished that the usually sensitive horse not only submitted to these caresses, but actually responded to the extent of affecting to nip my mistress's little right ear.

This was enough for the impulsive Consuelo. She ran hastily into the house, and in a few moments reappeared in a bewitching riding skirt gathered round her jimp waist. In vain Enriquez and myself joined in earnest entreaty: the horse was hardly broken for even a man's riding yet; the saints alone could tell what the nervous creature might do with a woman's skirt flapping at her side! We begged for delay, for reflection, for at least time to change the saddle—but with no avail! Consuelo was determined, indignant, distressingly reproachful! Ah, well! if Don Pancho (an ingenious diminutive of my Christian name) valued his horse so highly—if he were jealous of the evident devotion of the animal to herself, he would—But here I succumbed! And then I had the felicity of holding that little foot for one brief moment in the

hollow of my hand, of readjusting the skirt as she threw her knee over the saddle-horn, of clasping her tightly—only half in fear—as I surrendered the reins to her grasp. And to tell the truth, as Enriquez and I fell back, although I had insisted upon still keeping hold of the end of the riata, it was a picture to admire. The petite figure of the young girl, and the graceful folds of her skirt, admirably harmonized with Chu Chu's lithe contour, and as the mare arched her slim neck and raised her slender head under the pressure of the reins, it was so like the lifted velvet-capped toreador crest of Consuelo herself, that they seemed of one race.

"I would not that you should hold the riata," said Consuelo petulantly.

I hesitated—Chu Chu looked certainly very amiable—I let go. She began to amble towards the gate, not mincingly as before, but with a freer and fuller stride. In spite of the incongruous saddle the young girl's seat was admirable. As they neared the gate she cast a single mischievous glance at me, jerked at the rein, and Chu Chu sprang into the road at a rapid canter. I watched them fearfully and breathlessly, until at the end of the lane I saw Consuelo rein in slightly, wheel easily, and come flying back. There was no doubt about it; the horse was under perfect control. Her second subjugation was complete and final!

From: THE SPORT OF QUEENS

Dick Francis

I learned to ride when I was five, on a donkey.

I rode without a saddle, partly because it was a pet theory of my father's that riding bareback was the best way to learn balance, but mostly because there was, anyway, no saddle to fit her high bony back.

As soon as he saw me urging this long-suffering animal with more enthusiasm than style over a very small rail fence, my elder brother offered me the princely sum of sixpence if I could jump the fence sitting backwards. At that time I was saving all my pocket money to buy a toy farm, so this offer could not be ignored. I turned round awkwardly with my knees pressed hard into her flanks, pointed the donkey's head at the fence, and kicked:

The donkey started off, and I went head first over her tail.

When my brother could control his mirth at this event he collected the moke, who was fortunately too lazy to run away, and returned me to her back. We went through this programme twice more, and it became obvious that my brother's laughter was beginning to cause him considerable pain.

However, after a pause, during which I rubbed the parts of me which had hit the ground, and my brother rubbed his stomach, gasped for breath, and wiped the tears from his cheeks, we tried again.

He thought his sixpence was quite safe, but I wanted my farm very much.

This time I stayed on until the donkey jumped, but we landed on opposite sides of the fence.

Finally, with my nine-year-old brother shouting and chasing us with a waving stick, the donkey and I jumped the fence together, landed together, and came precariously to a halt.

The sixpence was solemnly handed over, and in this way I earned my first riding fee. In my heart, from that moment, I became a professional horseman.

From: RIDING LESSONS

Sara Gruen

"Are you ready?" says Roger as he gives me a leg up, and I laugh, because I've never been more ready in all my life.

And Harry is, too, with his red neck flexed and his ears swiveling like antennae, but never together—if one is forward the other is back, although sometimes they land impossibly out to the side, like a lop-eared goat's. He stamps and snorts as I lower myself into the saddle and gather the reins, and I forgive him, this time, for not standing still while I mount, because while it's terrible manners, there are extenuating circumstances and I, too, cannot be still. I run the reins across the black gloves that cover my wet palms and icy fingers, and look back at my father, whose face is lined and stern, and then at Roger, who smiles up at me with his face a perfect composite of tension, pride, and joy.

He lays a hand on my booted calf and says, "Give 'em hell, Babe," and I laugh again, because I have every intention of doing just that.

And then Marjory is leading us to the gate—actually holding the reins, as though I can be trusted to take fences of almost five feet but not to steer Harry into the arena.

"Watch your pace going into the combination," she says, "and don't let him rush you. Collect him sharply coming around the turn after the water jump, and if you get past the oxer and you're still clear, hold him back and take it easy because you've already got it even if you take a time fault."

I nod and look across at the judges because I know that already. We can take eight faults and still tie for first, and if we get none or four we've done it, and nobody else has a hope. Marjory is still talking and I nod impatiently and just want to start because Harry and I are going to explode with the excitement of it all, and we're ready, we're ready, oh, we're ready. But I know it's not Marjory who gets to decide so I try to remember to breathe and ignore her and suddenly it's easy, as though I'm in a wind tunnel and all of everything beyond Harry and me is on the outside.

Then I get the signal and I think that it's time to go—think it, that's all—and Harry goes, walking forward so deep on the bit his nose is pressed to his chest, and as we step into the arena I can see our shadow on the ground and his tail on end like a flag. The man on the PA introduces us—Annemarie Zimmer on Highland Harry, with a commanding lead and yadda yadda yadda, but no one's paying attention, because they're staring at Harry. No gasps or murmurs this time, not on day three, but then someone goes and wrecks it because I hear some bastard man say, "Now there goes a horse of a different color," and I know from that one remark that he's missed days one and two and I hate him because I know he feels clever for the remark. But I suppose I'd say it too, since you don't see many or any striped horses out there, and before Harry I never knew such a thing existed, but here he is, and there's no denying that. Not today. Not here.

I hear the whistle and press my calves against him and we're off. Harry shoots forward like a coiled spring, so compressed his haunches feel like they're right under me.

I tighten my fingers, No, no, no Harry, not yet, I'll let you, but not yet, and his ears prick forward, together this time, and he says All right, and gives me a collected canter that feels like a rocking horse, so high on the up and so low on the down. And we rock around the corner and approach the first jump and he asks me, Now? And I say, No, and he says Now? And I say No, and then a stride later I can tell he's about to ask again, but before he can I say Yes, and he's off and I don't have to do anything else—won't have to until we're over and on the other side, and then I'll just have to ask him again, and he'll do it because he loves me and we're one.

There's the flap-flap-flap of leather on leather, the heavy incalzando of hoof-beats, da-da-da, da-da-*da*, da-da-*da*, and then a massive push, a hundred thousand compressed pounds exploding forth before—

Silence. As we arc over the fence, the only parts of me in contact with anything are my calves and hands and the balls of my feet although it looks like I'm lying on him, so forward am I and curved

around his neck with my face alongside where his mane would be if it weren't braided into a row of nubby topknots. And then *bang*! We've landed, and as soon as his front hooves make contact with the ground I'm back in the saddle and we're headed toward the brick wall and it's perfect. I can tell we're going to be clear because that's just the way it is.

We're flying now, and it's a wonder to me that we touch the ground at all because clearly we don't need to over one, two, three more fences. I lose remembrance of the order of it but don't need to remember because I feel it, looked at it until it became a part of my being, and here we are at the spread now, where White Night and Frito Misto both refused, but not Harry—on and past, to the water, and I'm letting him now, trusting him, and we're flying. I bring him in on the turn, just like Marjory said, and now we're headed for the double oxer, only the combination left between us and the finish, and if we clear just one more, the ribbon is in the bag and we're off to the Rolex-Kentucky, and who knows, maybe the Olympics, because why not? Because anything and everything is possible.

Let me, he says, and I say Yes, because how can I not, and I feel the energy gather in his haunches and then *pow*! He shoots us off the ground and the crest of his neck rises toward me and I thrust my hands forward to keep the reins light and it's beautiful. I catch a glimpse of a few faces over the boards in the spectator stands and I know they're rooting for us, holding their breath—even Dan, who is out there although he's still mad about Roger—and the moment I feel Harry's hind hocks clear the top I know we've done it. We've taken first place, and although we're still air-bound I'm rejoicing because we've done it, and it can't be taken away.

From: THE STORY OF THE LAKE

Laura Chester

The lead horse crashed into the stream and all the others followed, lurching through the water. Helen gave a shout as Shadow sank up to his belly. Sprays of water soaked her boots and the calves of her jodhpurs. Alicia Bosquet lifted her black boots together, while Helen's pony paused mid-stream to violently paw water on her horse's face. Joseph laughed at the impertinence, but Alicia, quite alarmed, bent to scold the youngest rider. "What are you doing there? Can't you move that pony on!" As they rose onto the bank, scrambling through briars, mud was flying, and the men were shouting that they had him now, had the fox securely on this two-mile island, and Helen wondered if she would actually see the kill. There was such gleeful confusion as the horses clashed together, men and horses pushing up against each other there on dry land.

Heinrich split them into groups, waving to both Helen and Joseph to follow him as one party headed off around the north end of the island, another to the south. They took the trail that cut across the island, though it looked less well maintained. Branches whipped at their faces, and Helen had to shield her eyes. Kicking to keep up with him, she cropped Shadow on, for Joseph was right behind her. They took a sharp right just as the trail dipped down, and she saw a slim birch tree had fallen across the path. Mr. Ulrich yelled a warning, "Heads up!" as Tyack took the jump, but the log lay up to Shadow's shoulder, and though the pony's heart sailed into it, and Helen leaned forward with all good intention, her mother's warning pulled her back with just enough hesitation, so that the pony's hoof caught upon the slick white bark—she felt herself plowing, her left hand out, heard the thud of the animal on the hard ground beside her, felt the snap in her thumb before she struck full force, crushing the wind from her chest with a cry that was a slap of both pain and stupidity—rolling backward on the ground, all of this in an instant—as Joseph's lathered girth flew over her.

From: IN PRAISE OF HORSES
Mark Spragg

In the afternoons I handled the colts; I gentled them by routine. I haltered them. I ran my hands along their necks, under their bellies. I pinched their flanks. I lifted their tails. Checked their teeth. Spoke to them. I swatted their rumps, and withers, and backs, and legs with an empty gunnysack. They shied, and snorted, and turned and came to realize that they were not harmed. I bridled them. Led them. Saddled them. I reminded them that we were put together to serve.

There were times when I swung into the saddle and a young horse would rise into the air and to earth again, and again, twisting, grunting, screaming his frustrations, bent on divorce from me. If I did not come loose he would finally spend himself, stand quivering, sweating his hot, sweet scent. I would shift my weight, step him out, work him in circles. I would slap his neck with a short, flat quirt to reinforce the pressure of the reins. First one way, and then the other. I would stop him. Start him. I would feel smaller for his loss of recklessness.

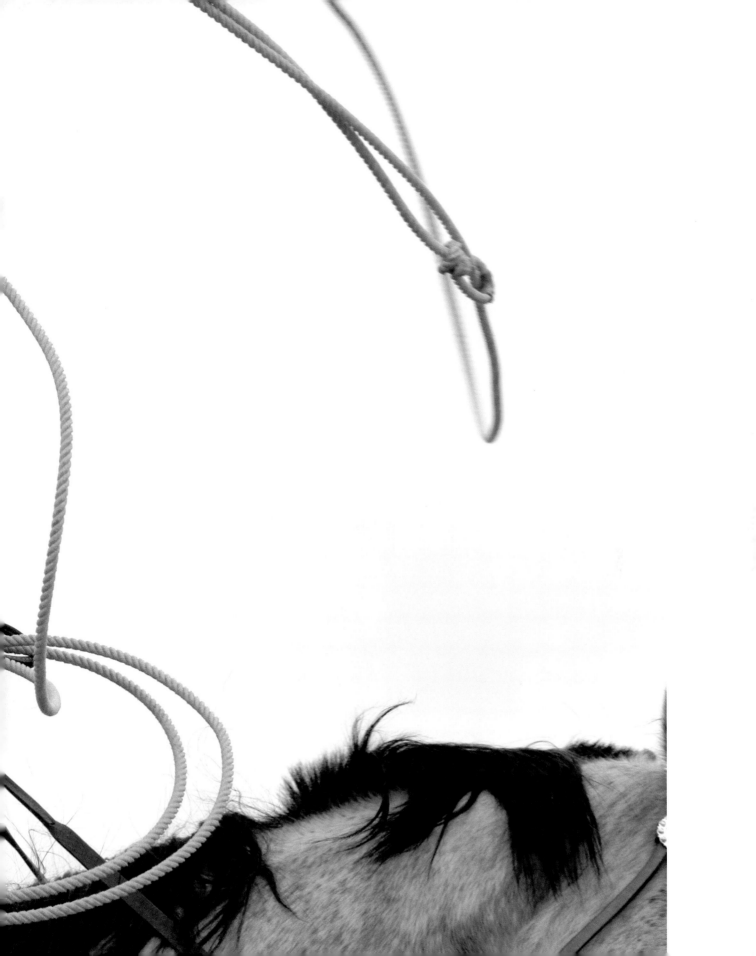

From: THE VIRGINIAN

Owen Wister

Some notable sight was drawing the passengers, both men and women, to the window; and therefore I rose and crossed the car to see what it was. I saw near the track an enclosure, and round it some laughing men, and inside it some whirling dust, and amid the dust some horses, plunging, huddling, and dodging. They were cow ponies in a corral, and one of them would not be caught, no matter who threw the rope. We had plenty of time to watch this sport, for our train had stopped that the engine might take water at the tank before it pulled us up beside the station platform of Medicine Bow. We were also six hours late, and starving for entertainment. The pony in the corral was wise, and rapid of limb. Have you seen a skilful boxer watch his antagonist with a quiet, incessant eye? Such an eye as this did the pony keep upon whatever man took the rope. The man might pretend to look at the weather, which was fine; or he might affect earnest conversation with a bystander: it was bootless. The pony saw through it. No feint hoodwinked him. This animal was thoroughly a man of the world. His undistracted eye stayed fixed upon the dissembling foe, and the gravity of his horse-expression made the matter one of high comedy. Then the rope would sail out at him, but he was already elsewhere; and if horses laugh, gayety must have abounded in that corral. Sometimes the pony took a turn alone; next he had slid in a flash among his brothers, and the whole of them like a school of playful fish whipped round the corral, kicking up the fine dust, and (I take it) roaring with laughter. Through the window-glass of our Pullman the thud of their mischievous hoofs reached us, and the strong, humorous curses of the cowboys. Then for the first time I noticed a man who sat on the high gate of the corral, looking on. For he now climbed down with the undulations of a tiger, smooth and easy, as if his muscles flowed beneath his skin. The others had all visibly whirled the rope, some of them even shoulder high. I did not see his arm lift or move. He appeared to hold the rope down low, by his leg. But like a sudden

snake I saw the noose go out its length and fall true; and the thing was done. As the captured pony walked in with a sweet, church-door expression, our train moved slowly on to the station, and a passenger remarked, "That man knows his business."

FROM: THE WILDERNESS HUNTER

Theodore Roosevelt

I started in the bright sunrise, riding one horse and driving loose before me eight others, one carrying my bedding. They travelled strung out in single file. I kept them trotting and loping, for loose horses are easiest to handle when driven at some speed, and moreover the way was long. My rifle was slung under my thigh; the lariat was looped on the saddle-horn.

At first our trail led through winding coulies, and sharp grassy defiles; the air was wonderfully clear, the flowers were in bloom, the breath of the wind in my face was odorous and sweet. The patter and beat of the unshod hoofs, rising in half-rhythmic measure, frightened the scudding deer; but the yellow-breasted meadow larks, perched on the budding tops of the bushes, sang their rich full songs without heeding us as we went by.

When the sun was well on high and the heat of the day had begun we came to a dreary and barren plain, broken by rows of low clay buttes. The ground in places was whitened by alkali; elsewhere it was dull gray. Here there grew nothing save sparse tufts of coarse grass, and cactus, and sprawling sage brush. In the hot air all things seen afar danced and wavered. As I rode and gazed at the shimmering haze the vast desolation of the landscape bore on me; it seemed as if the unseen and unknown powers of the wastes were moving by and marshalling their silent forces. No man save the wilderness dweller knows the strong melancholy fascination of these long rides through lonely lands.

From: BUCKING HORSES AND RIDERS

Will James

Nobody gets credit for riding easy in a rocking-chair. What the cowboy wants is a head-fighting, limber-back cross between greased lightning and where it hits—a horse that'll call for all the endurance, main strength, and equilibrium that cowboy's got—just so he can show his ability and scratch both ways from the cinch, as the judges may direct. There's when a mean devil of a horse is wanted; he gets a chance to show how mean he is with free rein, and the cowboy has something worth while to work at.

I've knowed some great horses in that game—there was Long Tom, Hammerhead, Old Steamboat; that last was a great old pony, eleven hundred pounds of solid steel and action and a square shooter. They say he never was rode, but I know he has been rode to a standstill. They was real riders that did it, tho'. I figgered that horse was part human the way he'd feel out his rider. He'd sometimes try him out on a few easy jumps just to see how he was setting, and when he'd loosen up for the last, it's safe enough to say, when that last would come and the dust cleared, there'd 'most always be a tall lean lanky bow-legged cowboy picking himself up and wondering how many horses he'd seen in the last few seconds. I've seen Old Steamboat throw his man with his head up and four feet on the ground, but what happened before he got in that peaceful position was enough to jar a centipede loose—and a human's only got two legs.

From: LORNA DOONE

R.D. Blackmore

"Your mare," said I, standing stoutly up, being a tall boy now; "I never saw such a beauty, sir. Will you let me have a ride of her?"

"Think thou couldst ride her, lad? She will have no burden but mine. Thou couldst never ride her. Tut! I would be loath to kill thee."

"Ride her!" I cried with the bravest scorn, for she looked so kind and gentle; "there never was a horse upon Exmoor foaled, but I could tackle in half an hour. Only I never ride upon saddle. Take them leathers off of her."

He looked at me with a dry little whistle, and thrust his hands into his breeches-pockets, and so grinned that I could not stand it. And Annie laid hold of me in such a way that I was almost mad with her. And he laughed, and approved her for doing so. And the worst of all was—he said nothing.

"Get away, Annie, will you? Do you think I'm a fool, good sir! Only trust me with her, and I will not override her."

"For that I will go bail, my son. She is liker to override thee. But the ground is soft to fall upon, after all this rain. Now come out into the yard, young man, for the sake of your mother's cabbages. And the mellow straw-bed will be softer for thee, since pride must have its fall. I am thy mother's cousin, boy, and am going up to house. Tom Faggus is my name, as everybody knows; and this is my young mare, Winnie."

What a fool I must have been not to know it at once! Tom Faggus, the great highway-man, and his young blood-mare, the strawberry! Already her fame was noised abroad, nearly as much as her master's; and my longing to ride her grew tenfold, but fear came at the back of it. Not that I had the smallest fear of what the mare could do to me, by fair play and horse-trickery, but that the glory of sitting upon her seemed to be too great for me; especially as there were rumours abroad that she was not a mare after all, but a witch. However, she looked like a filly all over, and wonderfully beautiful, with her supple stride, and soft slope of shoulder, and glossy coat beaded with water, and promi-

nent eyes full of docile fire. Whether this came from her Eastern blood of the Arabs newly imported, and whether the cream-colour, mixed with our bay, led to that bright strawberry tint, is certainly more than I can decide, being chiefly acquaint with farm-horses. And these come of any colour and form; you never can count what they will be, and are lucky to get four legs to them.

Mr. Faggus gave his mare a wink, and she walked demurely after him, a bright young thing, flowing over with life, yet dropping her soul to a higher one, and led by love to anything; as the manner is of females, when they know what is the best for them. Then Winnie trod lightly upon the straw, because it had soft muck under it, and her delicate feet came back again.

"Up for it still, boy, be ye?" Tom Faggus stopped, and the mare stopped there; and they looked at me provokingly.

"Is she able to leap, sir? There is good take-off on this side of the brook."

Mr. Faggus laughed very quietly, turning round to Winnie so that she might enter into it. And she, for her part, seemed to know exactly where the fun lay.

"Good tumble-off, you mean, my boy. Well, there can be small harm to thee. I am akin to thy family, and know the substance of their skulls."

"Let me get up," said I, waxing wroth, for reasons I cannot tell you, because they are too manifold; "take off your saddle-bag things. I will try not to squeeze her ribs in, unless she plays nonsense with me."

Then Mr. Faggus was up on his mettle, at this proud speech of mine; and John Fry was running up all the while, and Bill Dadds, and half a dozen. Tom Faggus gave one glance around, and then dropped all regard for me. The high repute of his mare was at stake, and what was my life compared to it? Through my defiance, and stupid ways, here was I in a duello, and my legs not come to their strength yet, and my arms as limp as a herring.

Something of this occurred to him, even in his wrath with me, for he spoke very softly to the filly, who now could scarce subdue herself; but she drew in her nostrils, and breathed to his breath, and did all she could to answer him.

"Not too hard, my dear," he said; "let him gently down on the mixen. That will be quite enough." Then he turned the saddle off, and I was up in a moment. She began at first so easily, and pricked her ears so lovingly, and minced about as if pleased to find so light a weight upon her, that I thought she knew I could ride a little, and feared to show any capers. "Gee wugg, Polly!" cried I, for all the men were now looking on, being then at the leaving-off time; "Gee wugg, Polly, and show what thou be'est made of." With that I plugged my heels into her, and Billy Dadds flung his hat up.

Nevertheless, she outraged not, though her eyes were frightening Annie, and John Fry took a pick to keep him safe; but she curbed to and fro with her strong forearms rising like springs ingathered, waiting and quivering grievously, and beginning to sweat about it. Then her master gave a shrill clear whistle, when her ears were bent towards him, and I felt her form beneath me gathering up like whalebone, and her hind-legs coming under her, and I knew that I was in for it.

First she reared upright in the air, and struck me full on the nose with her comb, till I bled worse than Robin Snell made me; and then down with her fore-feet deep in the straw, and her hind-feet going to heaven. Finding me stick to her still like wax, for my mettle was up as hers was, away she flew with me swifter than ever I went before, or since, I trow. She drove full-head at the cob-wall—"Oh, Jack, slip off," screamed Annie—then she turned like light, when I thought to crush her, and ground my left knee against it. "Mux me," I cried, for my breeches were broken, and short words went the furthest—"if you kill me, you shall die with me." Then she took the courtyard gate at a leap, knocking my words between my teeth, and then right over a quick set hedge, as if the sky were a breath to her; and away for the water-meadows, while I lay on her neck like a child at the breast, and wished I had never been born. Straight away, all in the front of the wind, and scattering clouds around her, all I knew of the speed we made was the frightful flash of her shoulders, and her mane like trees in a tempest. I felt the earth under us rushing away, and the air left far behind us, and my breath came and went, and I prayed to God, and was sorry to be so late of it.

All the long swift while, without power of thought, I clung to her crest and shoulders, and dug my nails into her creases, and my toes into her flank-part, and was proud of holding on so long, though sure of being beaten. Then in her fury at feeling me still, she rushed at another device for it, and leaped the wide water-trough sideways across, to and fro, till no breath was left in me. The hazelboughs took me too hard in the face, and the tall dog-briers got hold of me, and the ache of my back was like crimping a fish; till I longed to give it up, thoroughly beaten, and lie there and die in the cresses. But there came a shrill whistle from up the home-hill, where the people had hurried to watch us; and the mare stopped as if with a bullet; then set off for home with the speed of a swallow, and going as smoothly and silently. I never had dreamed of such delicate motion, fluent, and graceful, and ambient, soft as the breeze flitting over the flowers, but swift as the summer lightning. I sat up again, but my strength was all spent, and no time left to recover it, and though she rose at our gate like a bird, I tumbled off into the mixen.

THE FORGE

Seamus Heaney

All I know is a door into the dark.
Outside, old axles and iron hoops rusting;
Inside, the hammered anvil's short-pitched ring,
The unpredictable fantail of sparks
Or hiss when a new shoe toughens in water.
The anvil must be somewhere in the centre,
Horned as a unicorn, at one end square,
Set there immovable: an altar
Where he expends himself in shape and music.
Sometimes, leather-aproned, hairs in his nose,
He leans out on the jamb, recalls a clatter
Of hoofs where traffic is flashing in rows;
Then grunts and goes in, with a slam and flick
To beat real iron out, to work the bellows.

AMANDA IS SHOD

Maxine Kumin

The way the cooked shoes sizzle
dropped in a pail of cold water
the way the coals in the portable forge
die out like hungry eyes
the way the nails go in aslant
each one the tip of a snake's tongue

and the look of the parings
after the farrier's knife
has sliced through.

I collect them
four marbled white C's
as refined as petrified wood
and dry them to circles of bone
and hang them away on my closet hook

lest anyone cast a spell on Amanda.

THE HORSE OF FASHION

Russell Edson

There was a horse wearing four high-heeled shoes made of iron. When the equestrian was asked about this he said that the blacksmith had assured him that this was the height of equine fashion.

When the horse was seen again it was wearing lipstick and false eyelashes.

When the equestrian was asked about this he said that the blacksmith had assured him that this was the latest thing in the world of equine fashion.

When the horse was seen again it was wearing a wedding gown.

When the equestrian was asked about this he said, we're getting married.

Oh, how nice; I suppose the blacksmith approves?

We plan to be married at the alter of his anvil.

From: THE GYPSIES

Jan Yoors

On the way back to the camp we came across several small groups of Gypsies, either going toward the hamlet or, like ourselves, returning from it. Some girls had gathered pinecones and branches for fires. Half-naked young children were playing and running along the dirt track, straying too far from the camp. We noticed that the numerous horses grazing about were getting frisky. They had been left untethered because the grass was sparse and this left them more field to graze on. They lifted their heads, twisted their ears and snorted. Without any hesitation we ran over to them to investigate. Kore caught two of them by the manes and brought them to me to hold by the braided rope halters while he tried to get another one, while several other boys and men ran to catch their own, sensing trouble but still ignoring the reasons for it. The horses breathed heavily, and Kore, who was with them more than I was, held on to the frisky stallion, which danced in a half circle around the barefoot boy. Its legs quivered with excitement and the taut veins stood out noticeably on the buttocks. As the wind shifted slightly, the horses pulled away in one direction like a frightened herd, pulling us along with them. They stopped to look back again and milled around in disarray while we hung heavily on the halters or onto the manes, trying to subdue them. Shading our eyes, we peered in the direction the animals seemed to be fleeing from, and they turned their heads toward the danger. Then a crackling, hissing sound caught our attention. It was immediately followed by a more ominous rumbling as of an oncoming storm but at ground level instead of in the sky. A brush fire was suddenly rushing toward us. We swung onto the horses' backs and with wild yells encouraged the herd to flee, directing it toward the camp instead of letting them simply scatter, which in their fear was their tendency. Our distant yells echoed throughout the entire camp, where most Gypsies had also seen the signs of danger. We hurriedly gathered all small children within easy reach and bundled them off with several young women, babies astride their hips or still nursing. Everywhere women hastily gathered their belongings and threw them into wagons already on the move. Pulika stayed behind and so did Keja. When we were a fair distance up the road, Kore and Putzina tried to ride back, straddling the stallion, but they could not force the frenzied animal in the direction of the fire. There was little smoke, but the heat could be felt even at a fair distance. Hordes of frightened game ran out of the brush, and loudly shrieking pheasants and partridges shot by in their uproarious and heavy flight.

From: HORSE PEOPLE

Michael Korda

For her, freedom and happiness would be forever defined by that moment, associated in some way with having your hands in a horse's mane, feeling its stride, and the sound of its hooves and breathing.

There wasn't anything formal about the way Margaret kept Snowy, or the way the friend she had made in Overbury, Nancy, kept *her* pony, Bess. Any moment they could, they simply pulled their ponies out of their fields, tacked them up, mounted, and galloped off. "All we did," Margaret says, "was throw a leg over and go." A certain amount of grooming took place—on the whole, little girls enjoy grooming a pony almost as much as the pony enjoys the attention—and an occasional stab at cleaning the tack, but that's about it. It's a heady thing—little girls are bossed around by almost everybody, but in the relationship between a little girl and a pony the little girl is the boss, or is supposed to be. And the pony is there, close at hand, part of the rural landscape, ready to go when she is, always happy to see her, visible in its field through the window even on rainy days when it's not going to be ridden—and it's hardly surprising that Margaret, like a lot of little girls, dreamed of marrying her pony (though an alternative ambition was to marry her dog).

From: HOW MR. PICKWICK UNDERTOOK TO DRIVE

Charles Dickens

'Bless my soul!' said Mr. Pickwick, as they stood upon the pavement while the coats were being put in. 'Bless my soul! who's to drive? I never thought of that.'

'Oh! you, of course,' said Mr. Tupman.

'Of course,' said Mr. Snodgrass.

'I!' exclaimed Mr. Pickwick.

'Not the slightest fear, sir,' interposed the hostler. 'Warrant him quiet, sir; a hinfant in arms might drive him.'

'He don't shy, does he?' inquired Mr. Pickwick. 'Shy, sir?—He wouldn't shy if he was to meet a vaggin-load of monkeys with their tails burnt off.'

'The last recommendation was indisputable. Mr. Tupman and Mr. Snodgrass got into the bin; Mr. Pickwick ascended to his perch, and deposited his feet on a floor-clothed shelf, erected beneath it for that purpose.

'Now, shiny Villiam,' said the hostler to the deputy hostler, 'give the gen'l'm'n the ribbins.' 'Shiny Villiam'—so called, probably, from his sleek hair and oily countenance—placed the reins in Mr. Pickwick's left hand; and the upper hostler thrust a whip in his right.

'Wo–o!' cried Mr. Pickwick, as the tall quadruped evinced a decided inclination to back into the coffee-room window.

'Wo–o!' echoed Mr. Tupman and Mr. Snodgrass, from the bin.

'Only his playfulness, gen'l'm'n,' said the head hostler encouragingly; 'jist kitch hold of him, Villiam.' The deputy restrained the animal's impetuosity, and the principal ran to assist Mr. Winkle in mounting.

'T' other side, sir, if you please.'

'Blowed if the gen'l'm'n worn't a gettin' up on the wrong side,' whispered a grinning post-boy to the inexpressibly gratified waiter.

Mr. Winkle, thus instructed, climbed into his saddle, with about as much difficulty as he would have experienced in getting up the side of a first-rate man-of-war.

'All right?' inquired Mr. Pickwick, with an inward presentiment that it was all wrong.

'All right,' replied Mr. Winkle faintly.

'Let 'em go,' cried the hostler—'Hold him in, sir,' and away went the chaise, and the saddle-horse, with Mr. Pickwick on the box of one, and Mr. Winkle on the back of the other, to the delight and gratification of the whole inn yard.

'What makes him go sideways?' said Mr. Snodgrass in the bin, to Mr. Winkle in the saddle.

'I can't imagine,' replied Mr. Winkle. His horse was drifting up the street in the most mysterious manner—side first, with his head towards one side of the way, and his tail towards the other.

Mr. Pickwick had no leisure to observe either this or any other particular, the whole of his facilities being concentrated on the management of the animal attached to the chaise, who displayed various peculiarities, highly interesting to a bystander, but by no means equally amusing to any one seated behind him. Besides constantly jerking his head up, in a very unpleasant and uncomfortable manner, and tugging at the reins to an extent which rendered it a matter of great difficulty for Mr. Pickwick to hold them, he had a singular propensity for darting suddenly every now and then to the side of the road, then stopping short, and then rushing forward for some minutes, at a speed which it was wholly impossible to control.

'What *can* he mean by this?' said Mr. Snodgrass, when the horse had executed this manoeuvre for the twentieth time.

'I don't know,' replied Mr. Tupman; 'it *looks* very like shying, don't it?' Mr. Snodgrass was about to reply, when he was interrupted by a shout from Mr. Pickwick.

'Woo!' said that gentleman; 'I have dropped my whip.'

'Winkle,' said Mr. Snodgrass, as the equestrian came trotting up on the tall horse, with his hat over his ears, and shaking all over, as if he would shake to pieces, with the violence of the exercise, 'pick up the

whip, there's a good fellow.' Mr. Winkle pulled at the bridle of the tall horse till he was black in the face; and having at length succeeded in stopping him, dismounted, handed the whip to Mr. Pickwick, and grasping the reins, prepared to remount.

Now whether the tall horse, in the natural playfulness of his disposition, was desirous of having a little innocent recreation with Mr. Winkle, or whether it occurred to him that he could perform the journey as much to his own satisfaction without a rider as with one, are points upon which, of course, we can arrive at no definite and distinct conclusion. By whatever motives the animal was actuated, certain it is that Mr. Winkle had no sooner touched the reins, than he slipped them over his head, and darted backwards to their full length.

'Poor fellow,' said Mr. Winkle, soothingly—'poor fellow—good old horse.' The 'poor fellow' was proof against flattery: the more Mr. Winkle tried to get near him, the more he sidled away; and, notwithstanding all kinds of coaxing and wheedling, there were Mr. Winkle and the horse going round and round each other for ten minutes, at the end of which time each was at precisely the same distance from the other as when they first commenced—an unsatisfactory sort of thing under any circumstances, but particularly so in a lonely road, where no assistance can be procured.

'What am I to do?' shouted Mr. Winkle, after the dodging had been prolonged for a considerable time. 'What am I to do? I can't get on him.'

'You had better lead him till we come to a turnpike,' replied Mr. Pickwick from the chaise.

'But he won't come!' roared Mr. Winkle. 'Do come, and hold him.'

Mr. Pickwick was the very personation of kindness and humanity: he threw the reins on the horse's back, and having descended from his seat, carefully drew the chaise into the hedge, less anything should come along the road, and stepped back to the assistance of his distressed companion, leaving Mr. Tupman and Mr. Snodgrass in the vehicle.

The horse no sooner beheld Mr. Pickwick advancing towards him with the chaise whip in his hand, than he exchanged the rotary motion in which he had previously indulged, for a retrograde movement of so

very determined a character, that it at once drew Mr. Winkle, who was still at the end of the bridle, at a rather quicker rate than fast walking, in the direction from which they had just come. Mr. Pickwick ran to his assistance, but the faster Mr. Pickwick ran forward, the faster the horse ran backward. There was a great scraping of feet, and kicking up of the dust; and at last Mr. Winkle, his arms being nearly pulled out of their sockets, fairly let go of his hold. The horse paused, stared, shook his head, turned round, and quietly trotted home to Rochester, leaving Mr. Winkle and Mr. Pickwick gazing on each other with countenances of blank dismay. A rattling noise at a little distance attracted their attention. They looked up.

'Bless my soul!' exclaimed the agonised Mr. Pickwick, 'there's the other horse running away!'

It was but too true. The animal was startled by the noise, and the reins were on his back. The result may be guessed. He tore off with the four-wheeled chaise behind him, and Mr. Tupman and Mr. Snodgrass in the four-wheeled chaise. The heat was a short one. Mr. Tupman threw himself into the hedge. Mr. Snodgrass followed his example, the horse dashed the four-wheeled chaise against a wooden bridge, separated the wheels from the body, and the bin from the perch: and finally stood stock still to gaze upon the ruin he had made.

From: AN EYE FOR HORSES

Nancy Marie Brown

Behind me I heard a rise in the conversation, then hoofbeats. The woman rode up on the darker horse and handed me her whip. I had seen other Icelanders ride with one, longer than a riding crop but a bit short for a dressage whip. This one had an engraved silver cap on its handle. I took it like I had expected it, and gave the horse a tap. Immediately he picked up a nice slow tolt, as if he'd been merely waiting for me to ask. It was a confident gait; His back felt soft and rounded and comfortable beneath me, his head was high, and his neck arched. His forelock blew back past his ears, and his dark mane rippled over my hands. He seemed to be enjoying himself, glad to be about, though not in any great hurry. I must have been smiling, for the woman looked at me and beamed. She said something I didn't catch, and suddenly we were cantering up the hill. The horse had a fine, rolling canter. At the crest, we resumed the tolt, turned, cantered up the near hill, and tolted back to the barnyard. The horse stopped easily next to its fellow, and we got off. The rain was picking up again. Someone took the two horses into the stable. Another suggested coffee, and we all dashed for the house.

* * *

The rain was still steady, but inside the barn it was warm and brightly lit and comforting. A raised center aisle separated two large pens full of horses, each haltered and clipped to a rail. They stirred and stamped when we entered, and I looked along their orderly ranks for Birkir. Amazingly, I picked him out at once, the light bay with a star, and walked down the aisle toward him feeling as if he were already mine. Sigrun approached him from the rear, and the horses parted, leaving room for me to step into the pen and join her. We stood at his flank, looking him over, and he turned his head to watch us, his neck arced high, his ears pricked with curiosity. He had a dark, liquid, inquisitive eye, soft and friendly. Unlike Elfa, he was completely at ease around us. He did not sidle away when I reached to pat him—on the contrary, he poked his nose forward, doglike, to the limits of his rope, as if looking for attention. I scratched behind his ears and ran my hand down his neck and along his smooth wide back. His mane and tail were thick and dark, his black stockings neat, his hooves well-shaped, his coat a glowing red. He seemed larger and sturdier than most Icelandics I'd seen, and it was clear he was in excellent health.

"He's beautiful," I said, and meant it. I was filled with desire, suddenly, to own this beast—filled with awe that it was possible to own a creature so fine, so alive—surprised that anyone would actually let me take him away.

Drumbeats

If you have it, it is for life. It is a disease for which there is no cure. You will go on riding even after they have to haul you onto a comfortable wise old cob, with feet like inverted buckets and a back like a fireside chair.

—Monica Dickens

From: THE SILVER BRUMBY

Elyne Mitchell

Everything he saw, every cliff and crag, every rock or grassy glade, he knew of old, and yet he saw them now with a new intensity. He had trained himself never to forget any feature of the country through which he went, and now each tor, each weathered rock, was stamped on his memory like a photograph, and if he had to gallop through that photograph—escaping from either man or horse—he knew exactly where he could place each hard, strong hoof, exactly where he could leap, exactly where he could twist and turn.

All the world was very quiet, high up there on the Range. It was rarely that any other horses, except Storm and his herd, ever came as high, and most animals were already heading lower, anyway, before the snow came.

They saw dingoes, and occasionally a red fox, his pelt thick and good for winter, would show up against the grey-green grass. Thowra noticed how busy the scurrying insects were, from the tiny ants to the great bright blue and red mountain grasshoppers—but he, too, knew that it was going to be a heavy winter. A great deal of snow would fall to cover the bones of an old creamy mare if she chose to die up there among the high-lifted peaks of the Range.

Though the sun was shining, the first day they were up on the Range, a faint, milky haze was spreading over the sky the next morning. Already there was the winter hush of expectancy in the air.

Thowra had still not found Bel Bel, so he headed up yet higher, that second day, leading his herd through the chill dawn. The quietness was intense, there was no bird call, no rustle of leaves, and up there, not even the sound of a creek. Nothing moved except the silent-footed herd.

Into this still, quiet world, through an opening in the rocks, high above and to one side, burst Bel Bel, galloping for her life.

In a flash, Thowra knew that a man, or men, were after her and that she had taken that particular very rough way through the Ramsheads, hoping that she would not lead her hunter to himself.

Quickly, Thowra and his herd made themselves invisible among rocks, and from his hiding-place Thowra watched. He could only see one man, on a big chestnut horse, a well-bred-looking horse, and Bel Bel—Bel Bel galloping like the old mare she was, tired and not so nimble, depending on her own cunning and courage, rather than on her speed.

Then Thowra did something that no wild horse could be expected to do and which all the stockmen for ever afterwards spoke of as just another example of the mysteriousness of Thowra—he left his hidden mares and went off swiftly and silently on a line that would take him just below Bel Bel. He aimed to reach a certain clear snowgrass platform among the rocks before she did.

In the centre of this clear snowgrass, when he knew the man on his galloping chestnut would be able to see him clearly, he reared up and screamed the wild, triumphant scream of a stallion glorying in his own strength.

The man pulled up his horse on its haunches and stared at the gleaming stallion. Then, just as Thowra knew he would, he forgot Bel Bel, dug his spurs into the chestnut's flanks, and went after him at racing speed.

Thowra switched round and led him right away from Bel Bel—and away from Golden and his own mares, too.

Perhaps that stockman had recognized Bel Bel as the mother of Thowra, but he could not have hoped that Thowra would try to save her as he had, because no man would have believed—till then—that a full-grown brumby stallion would remember his mother. Quite certainly that stockman would not have expected Thowra to draw him off and *then* lead him such a terrifying gallop as could only have been devised by the most cunning of minds.

Thowra was enjoying himself. This rock and snowgrass world was his world. Not far from here was the great granite overhang under which he had been born. This was the country Bel Bel and Mirri had loved so much, the country in which he and Storm had romped as foals, and later, as irresponsible young colts.

How well he knew it all, the wild, high land, where wedgetail eagles planed overhead, and dingoes howled to the moon at night, where a silver stallion could leap from rock to rock right to the top of a granite tor, and scream his defiance at the pursuing man.

So Thowra raced ahead of the man—and mocked him—so he had raced with Arrow and mocked him. Up and down the ribbon lanes of snowgrass that lay between the tors, he went leaping through tumbled rocks, or up and up a tor, jumping from block to block. And Bel Bel, who had stopped to watch, saw her son, as she had once known she would, galloping free and wild, with his silver mane and tail foaming in the cold sunlight, like the spray of a gleaming waterfall. She saw him in all his perfection, poised on the top of a tor, noble cream head thrown up, as his defiant cry rang out, a great strong-shouldered, deep-chested stallion, not a fault in him, not in his powerful quarters, nor his strong, clean legs; a silver horse against the sky, free and wild, never marked by saddle, or girth, or spur, his speed never checked by a bit.

For a while she lost sight of them, but after some minutes she saw Thowra galloping along a narrow, rocky ledge below the South Ramshead, then along a ridge against the skyline, mane and tail streaming out like spun silver.

Bel Bel trotted across the mountainside. She lost sight of them again and, tired out, thought she would make towards the sandy cave where she had put her cream foal to shelter from the storm, long ago. On and on she trotted until suddenly, as she was getting near the cave, she heard the thundering of hooves. Quickly she hid herself in among some rocks. Outlined against the milky clouds was the great overhang of granite under which Thowra had been born.

As she watched, Thowra, all cream and silver strength, cleft the air above that granite rock, leapt, and landed twelve feet below, on soft snowgrass that had been his first bed, barely checked, and went galloping on.

Bel Bel saw the man on the rock's edge, trying to pull his horse back on its haunches and stop, but his speed was too great. The chestnut hurtled over, pecked badly on landing. The man somersaulted off

and the horse went madly on. Stirrups flapping, reins trailing, he vanished into the trees below.

The man lay still for a while and then got slowly to his feet and started down the mountain. Bel Bel moved towards the cave, making no sound, leaving no track, and feeling supremely happy. The winter snows would come now, to cover the bones of an old mare. She had seen Thowra as she had always known he would be—a king of mountain horses.

From: FREE REIN

Laura Chester

The angel of the equestrians is with us again this morning, shining through benevolent weather. She has slipped into the quince for a change of dress, that ugly duckling of the apple family. When the horses get a whiff of that pungent sweetness, little wings in their mouths start pulsing and we glide. You may not believe in this angel of the equestrians, but she moves with us under the tall trees, she leads us through the darkness to the track. She is beautiful, just beautiful, if only we could hear her laugh, at the mention of—"A death wish to ride with us!" She knows there is no escape, that the quince will return, even if they're taken, even if you have to wait a year. She sits between the blue reins of the least best bet, leaving all the losers in the dust.

IN THE BLUE PEWTER AIR

Lyn Lifshin

Light rain. Inside the
barn, dark shapes
of horses, ghost
shapes in the blue
pewter air. In the rain,
perfume of clover
and hay. Hot walkers
cool horses, Ruffian's
groom cleans her
stall. Click of metal
shoes. Manure
and roses. Ruffian
thrusts her head
forward as if to
harness the day
as her groom goes
over her black
coat with a rub
rag, polishes her
to onyx. Ruffian
twists and flicks,
shifts her weight
in grey dampness
where later her
hoof prints
fill with rain

ON THAT DAY

Lyn Lifshin

it was as if she had
wings and then
the wings turned to
wax, were melting.
There was a hush,
seconds after the
wild cheers as
Ruffian edged
ahead. It was hot
and the roses were
dripping. The sun
kept on, as it did
with Icarus falling
from the sky on
melting wings. The
birds didn't stop.
When her jockey
pulled her up that
last night, everyone
who knew must
have covered
their eyes

SONG

Mary Koncel

One horse is humming a little horse song. We might say this horse is fat and happy, point to wet dapples and mane, undo a top button. The other horse is dead. Once a branch broke just before midnight. Once two brothers pressed their cheeks against frozen pond, giggling. It was November, no wind, no birds, no moment of sky. We think this horse is humming about branches and runaway boys in flannel caps, but we don't ask. The other horse is dead. It grazed nearby, stretched its neck for clover. And now this horse is humming a little horse song. Perhaps a simple song, short but lovely, or a song for thrashing hooves, the certain coming of grief. We might sit on a fence and convince ourselves that if horses don't want to remember, they won't. They will close their eyes, stand rump to rump, share only sunlight or shadow.

From: MY HORSES, MY TEACHERS
Alois Podhajsky

A special gift for adapting to all circumstances in life was demonstrated by the sixteen stallions of the Spanish Riding School when, after the triumphant tour to the United States and Canada in December 1950, they got into a heavy storm on the Atlantic Ocean that lasted for several days. The *American Importer* was a freighter of medium size. In a large square room under deck two rows of boxes were built in such a way that the horses were able to see each other across a narrow passage in the middle where luggage and food were piled. They were walked for exercise up and down this passage by their grooms. The boxes were large enough so that the stallions could lie down but of course not of the size of their boxes at home in Vienna in which they may turn and roll to their hearts' content. It was on purpose that these boxes on board the ship were of a smaller size, and they served that purpose well when the storm broke loose. At first the stallions were one after the other thrown off their feet but were not rolled about in the violent movements of the ship as much as they would have been in larger boxes. After a short while, however, the stallions had learned the trick. With their legs wide apart like any old salt they leaned against one of the walls of their boxes in order to stand more securely. Instinctively they developed a special technique to preserve balance in the rolling ship. When the box went up on the side where they could look out they made their necks long and stretched their heads out into the corridor in order to take the weight off their hindquarters, which stood much lower now. When the ship swung to the other side so that the hindquarters went up and head and neck became low they stiffened their forelegs under the increased weight and withdrew heads and necks as far as possible into the box. Coming down to this part of the ship the traveller was confronted with a strange sight. In the rhythm of the billowing sea the white necks stretched to the maximum into the corridor and disappeared again behind the wooden

partitions of the boxes while a row of other white necks appeared from the boxes on the opposite side.

Except for one resistant man, the entire team of the Spanish Riding School, riders and grooms, lay seasick in their cabins. This last courageous one tried to take care of the stallions as best he could. But at the sight of the white bodies swinging back and forth, up and down, he, too, felt odd. Everything around him seemed in dizzy motion. He fled from the stuffy stables and groaned: "My God, I cannot bear to look at them, I am getting seasick too!" This was the end of his resistance and the Lipizzaners remained the only members of the Spanish Riding School who weathered the storm safe and sound.

DON'T LET'S GO TO THE DOGS TONIGHT
Alexandra Fuller

That day Mum and I ride up into the foothills on game paths and tracks that the terrorists have used. These paths are already strangled with fresh growth, with the promise of a new rainy season coming, the quick green threads of creepers stretching over old, dry tracks, swallowing footpaths, and demonstrating how quickly this part of Africa would reclaim its wild lands if it were left untrodden. The horses struggle over rocks, their unshod hooves slipping against the hard ground as we climb ever higher into the mountains. Mum rides ahead on Caesar, her big bay Thoroughbred, an ex-trotter rescued from an abusive home and made ridable again under Mum's patient training. I am on my fat chestnut pony, Burma Boy, a bad-tempered and ill-behaved animal; bucking, bolting, kicking, and biting regularly—all of which, Dad says, is good for me. The dogs swarm, noses down, through the bush ahead of us, yelping with excitement when they put up a hare or mongoose and bounding hysterically through the bush if they catch sight of a duiker or wild pig.

By late morning, we are on the border of our farm in the high, thick bush, as close to Mozambique as I have ever been on a horse.

"Keep your eyes peeled for buffalo bean," says Mum.

I start to itch at once and look ahead nervously. Buffalo bean is a creeper boasting an attractive purple bloom in the spring, followed by a mass of beans that are covered in tiny velvet hairs, which blow off in the wind and can lodge in your skin. The hairs can stimulate a reaction so severe, so burning and persistent, that it has been known to send grown men mad, tearing into the bush in search of mud in which to roll to alleviate the torture. I am also compelled to crouch, my head pressed against Burma Boy's neck, to avoid the strong, elaborate webs that spread taut across our path. In the middle of these bright, tight webs there are big red- and yellow-legged spiders waiting hopefully for prey to fall. Burma Boy's ears are laced with the silvery threads.

Mum is following the native cattle trails, fresh manure and tracks and freshly disturbed bush; she pushes on and on, occasionally getting off her horse to inspect the ground and then riding on with more confidence. "They've gone this way. See?" The cows have stayed close to the springs that feed out of the mountains and run through these foothills to come down into the rivers in the heart of our farm.

"Look," says Mum fiercely, "bloody cows! Look!" She points at the damaged stream banks and kicks Caesar on with fresh determination, her face set in a scowl. The horses are straining, wet with sweat and frothing white under the tail and mane. Even the dogs have stopped following their noses and bounding ahead after wild game scents; they are beginning to follow closely on the horses' heels, tongues lolling. I say, "Are we nearly there yet?" I am starting to get thirsty and we have brought nothing with us to drink.

Mum says, "Stop whinging."

"I'm not whinging. I was just *saying*."

"Start looking for mombies."

The cattle that have stayed up this high are wild. As quickly as we cover their fresh tracks, they move on, staying ahead of us, out of sight and almost beyond earshot. Mum says, "I'm going to go around. You stay here, and catch them if they come down." She pushes Caesar forward into the thick bush with the dogs scrambling behind her, and soon disappears from sight. For a while I can hear her and the dogs as they make their way through the bush, and then there is silence. I hold my breath and listen. I am surrounded by the high, whining noise of insects—their frantic spring singing in dry grass—and by the occasional shriek of an invisible bird. Burma Boy puts his head down and starts to pull at the thin, bitter dry grass. It is very hot and still and I am enveloped in the salty steam sent up by Burma Boy as he sweats; my fingers sting against the leather reins and my eyes burn. Sweat drips down from my hatband and flies swarm onto our stillness to take advantage of the moisture, crawling over my eyes and lips until I swat them away. I am very thirsty now.

"Mu-um." My voice sounds high and thin in the heat.

I wait. There is no answer. I hold my breath and then call again, louder, "Mu-uum!" Still no answer. I look around, suddenly imagining that terrorists might crawl up on me at any moment and take me by surprise. I wonder where Mum has gone; she has the gun with her. I wonder if she will hear me if I am attacked by terrorists. I close my eyes and take a deep breath. What will Burma Boy do if we are suddenly surrounded by terrorists? Bolt, no doubt. And I will be scraped off on a tree and lie winded and wounded on the ground waiting for Mum to come and rescue me. I wonder how she would find me again in this thick bush. I'd be dead by then. Shot. Eyelids chopped off and fried, no ears, no lips. Dead. Burma Boy would be home. They would have a funeral for me, like the funeral we had for Olivia. They would say how brave I was. I start to cry. I would be buried, next to my fried eyelids, lips, and ears, in a little coffin. There would be a hump of fresh earth, crawling with earthworms, piled over me in the little settlers' cemetery. Tears streamed down my face. The *Umtali Post* will write a moving article about my death.

"Mum!" I shout, genuinely frightened.

Burma Boy throws up his head at my alarm.

"It's okay," I say shakily, crying and running my hand down his wet neck. "It's okay."

I start to imagine that perhaps Mum, Caesar, and the dogs have been caught by terrorists themselves. Maybe Mum is lying in a bloody puddle, eyelidless and lipless, with the dogs licking helplessly, lovingly at her lifeless hands. I will be brave at Mum's funeral. The *Umtali Post* will write an article about me, lost and alone in the bush, while my mother lay dead surrounded by her faithful dogs and loyal horse. I turn Burma Boy around. "Do you know the way home?" I ask, letting him have his head. But he, after looking around for a few moments, placidly puts his head down and starts to eat again.

It feels like a long time during which I alternated between quiet, dry panic and noisy, copious weeping before I hear Mum and the dogs coming through the bush. Mum is singing, like the herdsmen taking the cows to the dip, "Here dip-dip-dip-dip-dip! Dip, dip-dip-dip-dip dip!"

And in front of her there are a dozen multicolored cows, running with heads held high, wild and frightened, their eyes white-rimmed, their long, unruly horns slashing at the bush. Burma Boy throws up his head, startled, and shies. I pull up the reins. Mum says, "Get behind me."

I start to cry with relief at seeing her. "I thought you were lost."

"Out the way," she shouts, "out the way! Get behind!"

I pull Burma Boy around.

"Come on," says Mum, riding past me, "let's herd this lot down."

I say, "You were so long."

"Catch the cows as they come through."

But the cows are not used to being herded and are unwilling and frightened participants. They break loose frequently and Mum has to circle back to bring the herd into order. She has identified the leader, a tall-hipped ox with a very old, almost worn-through leather strap around his neck that once must have held a bell. All the cows are dripping with ticks: their ears are crusted with small red ticks and their bodies are bumped with the raised gray engorged adults, which look ready to drop off. Mum says, "If we can keep the leader going, the rest might follow." But it still takes us more than an hour to move the cows less than half a mile. I start to cry again.

"What's the matter now?" says Mum irritably.

"I'm thirsty," I cry, "I'm tired."

"Well, you go on home, then," says Mum. "I'm bringing these cows down."

"But I don't know the way."

"*Fergodsake*," says Mum between her teeth.

I start to cry even harder.

She says, "Give Burma Boy his head, he'll take you home."

But Burma Boy, given his head, is content to follow Caesar and graze happily at this leisurely pace. "Look, he won't go home."

"Then *ride* him."

I kick feebly. "I'm thirsty," I whine.

Mum is unrelenting. "So let's get these cows home. The sooner we get these cows home the sooner you'll have something to drink."

We ride on for two more hours. I slouch over in my saddle, letting myself rock lazily with Burma Boy's tread. I make no attempt to herd the cows.

Mum scowls at me with irritation: "*Ride* your bloody horse."

I flap my legs and pull weakly at the reins. "He won't listen."

"Don't be so bloody feeble."

Fresh tears spring into my eyes. "I'm not being feeble."

Mum says, "If you would help, we'd get home a lot sooner."

We ride on in hostile silence for another half hour or so. Then I say, "I think I have buffalo bean." I start to scratch fretfully. I am so thirsty that my tongue feels dry and cracking. "I'm going to faint, I'm so thirsty."

Mum circles back to catch a stray cow.

"Mu-uuum."

She isn't going to listen. It is no good. It is clear that I am not going to get home until the cows are safely fenced up in the home paddocks. I pull Burma Boy's head up and circle him back to the lagging cows, straggling at the rear of the herd. "Dip, dip-dip-dip-dip-dip," I sing, my voice dry on the hot air. "Dip, dip-dip-dip-dip-dip-dip."

One of the cows tries to run out of the herd and break for the bush. I dig my heels into Burma Boy's sides and spin him around, catching the cow before she can escape.

"That's it," says Mum. "That's better. Keep it up."

It takes until late afternoon to get the cows down to the home paddocks, by which time the cows' flanks are wet with sweat, their horn-heavy heads are low and swinging; they are tripping forward without thought of a fight. I have stopped sniveling, but am hunched over the front of my saddle trying not to think about how thirsty I am.

"There," says Mum, wiping sweat off her top lip as she shuts the gate behind the wild cows, "that's not a bad day's work."

I shrug miserably.

"Don't you think?"

"I s'pose."

Mum swings up on Caesar again and pats him on the rump. "You know, we're descended from cattle rustlers, you and me," she tells me, her eyes shining. "In Scotland, our family were cattle rustlers."

I think, *At least Scotland is cool. At least there are streams of fresh water to drink from. At least Scottish cows don't lead you into buffalo bean.*

From: THE TRAVELS OF BARON MUNCHAUSEN

Rudolf Erich Raspe

I remember a superb Lithuanian horse, which no money could have bought. He became mine by an accident, which gave me an opportunity of showing my horsemanship to a great advantage. I was at Count Przobossky's noble country-seat in Lithuania, and remained with the ladies at tea in the drawing room, while the gentlemen were down in the yard to see a young horse of blood which had just arrived from the stud. We suddenly heard a noise of distress; I hastened downstairs, and found the horse so unruly, that nobody durst approach or mount him. The most resolute horsemen stood dismayed and aghast; despondency was expressed in every countenance, when, in one leap, I was on his back, took him by surprise, and worked him quite into gentleness and obedience, with the best display of horsemanship I was master of. Fully to show this to the ladies, and save them unnecessary trouble, I forced him to leap in at one of the open windows of the tea-room, walked round several times, pace, trot, and gallop, and at last made him mount the tea-table, there to repeat his lessons in a pretty style of miniature which was exceedingly pleasing to the ladies, for he performed them amazingly well, and did not break either cup or saucer.

From: ST. MAWR

D.H. Lawrence

"Mother, they want to shoot St. Mawr," she said.

"I know," said Mrs. Witt, as calmly as if Lou had said tea was ready.

"Well—" stammered Lou, rather put out, "don't you think it cheek?"

"It depends, I suppose, on the point of view," said Mrs. Witt dispassionately, looking closely at her lips. "I don't think the English climate agrees with me. I need something to stand up against, no matter whether it's great heat or great cold. This climate, like the food and the people, is most always lukewarm or tepid, one or the other. And the tepid and the lukewarm are not really my line." She spoke with a slow drawl.

"But they're in the drawing-room, mother, trying to force me to have St. Mawr killed."

"What about tea?" said Mrs. Witt.

"I don't care," said Lou.

Mrs. Witt worked the bell-handle.

"I suppose, Louise," she said, in her most beaming eighteenth-century manner, "that these are your guests, so you will preside over the ceremony of pouring out."

"No, mother, you do it. I can't smile to-day."

"I can," said Mrs. Witt.

And she bowed her head slowly, with a faint, ceremoniously effusive smile, as if handing a cup of tea.

Lou's face flickered to a smile.

"Then you pour out for them. You can stand them better than I can."

"Yes," said Mrs. Witt. "I saw Mrs. Vyner's hat coming across the churchyard. It looks so like a crumpled cup and saucer, that I have been saying to myself ever since: *Dear Mrs. Vyner, can't I fill your cup?*— and then pouring tea into that hat. And I hear the Dean responding: *My head is covered with cream, my cup runneth over.*—That is the way they make *me* feel."

They marched downstairs, and Mrs. Witt poured tea with that devastating correctness which made Mrs. Vyner, who was utterly impervious to sarcasm, pronounce her "indecipherably vulgar."

But the Dean was the old bulldog, and he had set his teeth in a subject.

"I was talking to Lady Carrington about that stallion, Mrs. Witt."

"Did you say stallion?" asked Mrs. Witt, with perfect neutrality.

"Why, yes, I presume that's what he is."

"I presume so," said Mrs. Witt colourlessly.

"I'm afraid Lady Carrington is a little sensitive on the wrong score," said the Dean.

"I beg your pardon," said Mrs. Witt, leaning forward in her most colourless polite manner. "You mean stallion's score?"

"Yes," said the Dean testily. "The horse St. Mawr."

"The stallion St. Mawr," echoed Mrs. Witt, with utmost mild vagueness. She completely ignored Mrs. Vyner, who felt plunged like a specimen into methylated spirit. There was a moment's full stop.

"Yes?" said Mrs. Witt naïvely.

"You agree that we can't have any more of these accidents to your young men?" said the Dean rather hastily.

"I certainly do!" Mrs. Witt spoke very slowly, and the Dean's lady began to look up. She might find a loophole through which to wriggle into the contest. "You know, Dean, that my son-in-law calls me, for preference, *belle-mére*! It sounds so awfully English when he says it; I always see myself as an old grey mare with a bell round her neck, leading a bunch of horses." She smiled a prim little smile, *very* conversationally. "Well!" and she pulled herself up from the aside. "Now, as the bell-mare of the bunch of horses, I shall see to it that my son-in-law doesn't go too near that stallion again. That stallion won't stand mischief."

She spoke so earnestly that the Dean looked at her with round wide eyes, completely taken aback.

"We all know, Mrs. Witt, that the author of the mischief is St. Mawr himself," he said, in a loud tone.

"Really! you think *that*?" Her voice went up in American surprise. "Why, how *strange*—!" and she lingered over the last word.

"Strange, eh?—After what's just happened?" said the Dean, with a deadly little smile.

"Why, yes! Most strange! I saw with my own eyes my son-in-law pull that stallion over backwards, and hold him down with the reins as tight as he could hold them; pull St. Mawr's head backwards on to the ground, till the groom had to crawl up and force the reins out of my son-in-law's hands. Don't you think that was mischievous on Sir Henry's part?"

The Dean was growing purple. He made an apoplectic movement with his hand. Mrs. Vyner was turned to a seated pillar of salt, strangely dressed up.

"Mrs. Witt, you are playing on words."

"No, Dean Vyner, I am not. My son-in-law pulled that horse over backwards and pinned him down with the reins."

"I am sorry for the horse," said the Dean, with heavy sarcasm.

"I am *very*," said Mrs. Witt, "sorry for that stallion: *very*!"

Here Mrs. Vyner rose as if a chair-spring had suddenly propelled her to her feet. She was streaky pink in the face.

"Mrs. Witt," she panted, "you misdirect your sympathies. That poor young man—in the beauty of youth!"

"Isn't he *beautiful*—" murmured Mrs. Witt, extravagantly in sympathy. "He is my daughter's husband!" And she looked at the petrified Lou.

"Certainly!" panted the Dean's wife. "And you can defend that—that—"

"That stallion," said Mrs. Witt. "But you see, Mrs. Vyner," she added, leaning forward female and confidential, "if the old grey mare doesn't defend the stallion, who will? All the blooming young ladies will defend my beautiful son-in-law. You feel so *warmly* for him yourself! I'm an American woman, and I always have to stand up for the accused. And I stand up for that stallion. I say it is not right. He was pulled over backwards and then pinned down by my

son-in-law—who may have meant to do it, or may not. And now people abuse him.—Just tell everybody, Mrs. Vyner and Dean Vyner"—she looked round at the Dean—"that the *belle-mère's* sympathies are with the stallion."

THE HORSES

Ted Hughes

I climbed through woods in the hour-before-dawn dark.
Evil air, a frost-making stillness,

Not a leaf, not a bird,—
A world cast in frost. I came out above the wood

Where my breath left tortuous statues in the iron light.
But the valleys were draining the darkness

Till the moorline—blackening dregs of the brightening grey—
Halved the sky ahead. And I saw the horses:

Huge in the dense grey—ten together—
Megalith-still. They breathed, making no move,

With draped manes and tilted hind-hooves,
Making no sound.

I passed: not one snorted or jerked its head.
Grey silent fragments

Of a grey silent world.

I listened in emptiness on the moor-ridge.
The curlew's tear turned its edge in the silence.

Slowly detail leafed from the darkness. Then the sun
Orange, red, red erupted

Silently, and splitting to its core tore and flung cloud,
Shook the gulf open, showed blue,

And the big planets hanging—
I turned

Stumbling in the fever of a dream, down towards
The dark woods, from the kindling tops,

And came to the horses.
                              There, still they stood,
But now steaming and glistening under the flow of light,

Their draped stone manes, their tilted hind-hooves
Stirring under a thaw while all around them

The frost showed its fires. But still they made no sound.
Not one snorted or stamped,

Their hung heads patient as the horizons,
High over valleys, in the red levelling rays—

In din of the crowded streets, going among the years, the faces,
May I still meet my memory in so lonely a place

Between the streams and the red clouds, hearing curlews,
Hearing the horizons endure.

THE VIEW FROM THE PASTURE

Dan Gerber

The old horse walks to the edge of the
pasture and stands stretching his neck
over the fence, as if he could see through
the falling snow, smell the ungrazed
grass matted under the ice or the frozen
orchard across the road.

There is no color in the earth or sky.
Viewing his world so long from this ground,
he knows the past and future was a windmill,
a tractor, a pump arm that beckons.

From: SWEET WILLIAM

John Hawkes

A bed of roses, the lawn, the gravel path leading to the veranda. And there at the foot of the mulberry, Molly's grave. It was twice the size at least of a human's grave, and it lay where Jane had demanded that it be dug, at the foot of her favorite tree and in full view of the house. My poor dam's grave, and only an immense rectangle of seething mud. And that, it came to me all at once, was the horror. For it was churning, that muddy earth, was moving, giving way to some terrible exertion in its very depths. This was the sound I heard, the agitation from which I could not escape. Even as I watched, wet and shivering, jaws set, eyes starting, heart aflame, suddenly a great hoof broke the surface, poked up, atop a dripping foreleg thrust itself upward, kicking this way and that, like some unnatural plant painfully and instantaneously flowering to full size. It jerked and twitched, that awful hoof, then came another, and another, and the fourth, all flaying the air and splattering the surrounding earth with watery gouts of red mud. Molly was rising! Molly, my dear dam, was climbing from her grave in the dawn light, heaving herself up, thrashing about, and I saw her head, the clotted eyes and nostrils, the haunches and the sodden tail. Up she rose, still blind, fighting for breath—my dead dam trying desperately to breathe!—and staggered forth, free at last of the torn and gaping pit.

My agony was exactly this, that in my young mind my dam was dead while the sight before my eyes told me that quite to the contrary she was coming back to me. Alive. I feared her muddied figure, how could I not? To flee from it was my only thought. But that muddied hulk was Molly, and I loved her and might well have dashed forth whinnying in fearful triumph at her return. But I only hid and waited behind the rhododendron, because now the great spraddle-legged creature shook herself and weakly, valiantly, started forward. Horrified I watched as Molly dragged herself up the gravel path, reached the veranda, and with her front feet managed to climb the first three steps toward the broad space where the Gordons spent their summer evenings laughing and softly talking together. There, half up the steps, half down, helpless to either proceed or retreat, there in all her covering of cold slime stood the dripping figure of my dam. She could not have been more pathetic, more grotesque.

She made no sound that I could hear, or remember hearing. Yet in some way she must have called to Jane, because suddenly Jane appeared in the screened door, came out and, wrapped only in a cool negligee, found her favorite mare not dead and underground, which had been grief enough, but risen, assuredly, and now balked in the poor animal's efforts to climb the veranda steps and enter the house. The sight was a shock too great for our generally cheerful Jane. She screamed, she rushed forward without the slightest hesitation and flung her arms around Molly's neck. From where I stood, small Jane looked as if she too had climbed from Molly's grave, horse and woman bonded together in the gluey stuff of common clay.

From: BARN BLIND

Jane Smiley

Peter, whose focus had narrowed considerably, almost totally, saw nothing but MacDougal; Mac he saw with a depth of field that was exhaustive and crystal clear. He had come to function as the perfect pivot point between the voice of his mother and the energies of his horse. Twenty-one hours a day he seemed about normal. He did his share of the work and the joking and the squabbling. He flirted absentmindedly with the girls, giving the usual impression that he wasn't aware of flirting, and therefore having great success. But his mind, more than ever, was on something else (and his mind had dwelt on many other things than the business at hand for as long as anyone could remember). It was on MacDougal.

During riding class he had usually, at least more than any other time, paid attention. Now, however, his attention was ferocious and continual and inarticulate; he could not be said to be thinking about riding, if "thinking" was to imply something to do with words. Although he read the anatomy book and memorized the terms, although he read the other books mother assigned him, and then answered her questions when she quizzed him during their afternoons together, and although her endless flow of talk was as the air itself, he understood nothing in terms of words and everything in terms of the way his bones and muscles and eyes and hands encountered the horse.

"Think of the cannon bone," said Kate. He was trotting around the warm-up ring. He thought of the cannon bone—straight from knee to ankle, simple, solid, guyed with ligaments and tendons. "What is the cannon bone doing now?" said Kate. "And what is the cannon bone doing now?" (He halted, he cantered forward, he took a small fence. MacDougal's four cannon bones flashed rhythmically and dependably in the sunlight.) And the cannon bone was by far the simplest of them all. The hoof, for example, was enough to boggle the mind. He hardly heard her questions, hardly heard his own answers, but their effect was to etch the drawings he had looked at into his memory, and further, to endow them with movement and meaning. These days MacDougal amazed him.

Success, compared to this—that is, the success of blue ribbons and praise from ex-members of the Team—was laughably irrelevant, and yet to all appearances he was bent on exactly that sort of success, and it was clear even to him that it would be forthcoming.

To John it was even clearer. Teddy groaned and farted and schemed for snatches of grass that showed green at the corners of his bits, looking untidy. He rubbed his enormous head against fenceposts and passersby, pulling strap ends out of their keepers and disarranging his bridle. He closed his eyes, hung his head, and resembled a plow horse. He rubbed John's careful braid out of his tail, breaking the hairs and making it impossible to rebraid. Everything that was done had to be done over. Nothing that was done enhanced Teddy's looks, and so nothing that was done brought esthetic pleasure. John smacked him with his hand, berated him, vented upon him the full force of his exasperation. Astride he had formed the habit of covert but abandoned vehemence, and it was an intoxicating habit.

During every lesson, John's turn came right after Peter's. In every group movement, he was to keep his eyes on MacDougal's beautiful hindquarters and silky tail, to keep his distance, but not to lag behind. After Peter galloped over a short jump course in perfect style and balance, he was to do the same. It was clear he could not hope to do better. How, he thought, had Peter, who had been just another of them two months before, grown so fair and golden, so graceful and precise, in a mere number of days? How did days add up in this way?

John spurred Teddy and held him in. The horse arched his neck and approached for a moment the condition of having flair. The horse lagged. If mother wasn't looking, John fluttered his whip, a proscribed behavior because it made horses whip shy, and, eventually, insensitive; the horse perked up. Peter made no mistakes. He held his hands low and quiet. He indicated gait and directional changes by a shift of weight. The small of his back, always within John's purview, flexed like a bow. His shoulders floated, his neck floated, his chin floated, his horse floated. His hair ruffled in the breeze, he was fair and beautiful. John had only two choices: to love his brother and hate himself, or to hate his brother and love himself. Mother shouted at him to pay attention, for goodness' sake, he was sticking his chin out from here to Buffalo. He realigned himself with a start, and Kate considered, with pardonable pride, that her judgment about Teddy had been just right. John was definitely shaping up, yes indeed. She smiled.

THE WHITE HORSE

D.H. Lawrence

The youth walks up to the white horse, to put its halter on
and the horse looks at him in silence.
They are so silent they are in another world.

From: THE CRAZY HUNTER

Kay Boyle

"And to think," the groom's voice went on as he came booted and clopping behind, "it was me that begun this, started you off that night in the paddocks when you had him out with me— If I was to do the right thing by everybody, you and the horse included, what I'd do now is tell Mrs. Lombe what's going on, get 'er up out-a-wer bed no matter if it's middle of the night or tomorrow morning, and she'd put 'er foot down and seen it was put a stop to. If I was to do what I ought to be doing now instead of—" He took one hand out of his mackintosh pocket and wiped the rain down his cheeks the way a comedian pretends to wipe the smile from his face, and then he started running clumsily forward through the mud and rain, stumbling ahead until he got to the horse's evenly and rhythmically riding croup and passed it, and then kept abreast the stirrup with the girl's plaid wool bedroom slipper thrust soaking in it while he said: "If I was to go to the house now and tell Mrs. Lombe, she wouldn't stand for it. She'd put a stop to it all right before anything worse came to happen, jumping on a stone-blind horse the way you say on a night that even frogs would stay home in. If I was to go back to the house now and get—"

"Only you wouldn't," the girl said, riding straight ahead. "You wouldn't do it because I need you to stand at the thirty-foot mark. If you didn't stand there, then something might happen because I couldn't judge close enough when to give him the rise. I worked it out from the book that maybe he'll jump this way if he won't jump any other. I wouldn't ask it for any other horse but just give him his rein and let him take off when he liked, maybe not elegant, according to the book, but that's the way I've always done it. The book says—"

"Oh, the book!" said Apby. Either she halted the horse or he halted of himself, but her voice and his movement ceased at the same instant and the groom looked up and, understanding what it was now, went ahead to open the paddock gate. She heard the hinges cry out and, waiting, heard Apby beginning the same arguments over in the same vexed, grieved tone.

"You can't do it no more than anybody could do it, a trainer couldn't do it and no book can tell you how to take a blind, dumb, unwitting, unwilling beast—" and she leaned forward and patted the horse's shoulder on which the rain poured like sweat.

"So you wouldn't let me down," she said as she rode in past Apby. "You'll stand at the thirty-foot mark where I made it this morning. I'll show it to you."

"Anyways," Apby said, letting the gate swing back, "if he breaks his back at it that'll be all right. They'll have to put him down tomorrow then, Mr. Penson or no Mr. Penson."

"Stand here, Apby," she said, bringing the horse to a halt in the grass. "Stand here. You can feel the bricks making a cross. That's it."

"You can't do it," Apby said again, and out of the little distance she had ridden away already, she said:

"I have done it. I did it alone with him over the knife-rest when there was moonlight, ten, fifteen times back and forth. The only difference is neither of us can see tonight. You stay where you are." The rain came quickly, quietly down, not in voluble articulation as on a house's roof or windows, but striking the face, the naked hands in silence, dropping steadily, as if forever, on the head and shoulders, the bent legs, beating softly as a moth's wings in the trees, until it was rain no longer after a while but the accumulated presence of water, more salient than the dark's or any human presence, like the presence of a vast and swiftly flowing, unseen river passage within arm's reach through the night. Apby stood with water trickling from his cap's stuff down across his face, water dripping unceasingly from the now lowered beak, one drop following another in rivulation to the corners of his mouth, into his ears until, like a bather, he put his forefingers into the ears' orifices and wrung them. "Damn the rain," was the last thing he heard her say before he heard the horse coming, and then a little later, either in imagination or in reality, saw coming towards him the dim cantering shape.

"She might have picked any other night to do it," he said half aloud, as if speaking to someone standing there with him for comfort's sake or else to split the blame with. He ran the back of his hand along his upper lip, under his water-beaded nose, and shook the drops off, and now the splatter of the horse's feet, the wind and thrash of his coming was almost ready to pass. He felt the movement of the air, the breath, the throb, heard even the saddle's creaking leather and the tossed bit's jangle, as if someone had opened a window or pushed open a door near him to let in these sounds he had not heard before in a vast darkened and silenced hall; and as the thing rushed past he leapt back and called the words out. "One, two, three!" he called out like a man crying desperately out from shore into the hopeless dark and wind to the floundered and drowning lost in a storm-pounded sea.

Mr. Sheehan, she thought for an instant, said that time in Florence that nobody should start riding too young, children being either too bold or too timid or both at the same time, and then the bold ones crack up going fast and they've no nerve left to go on the rest of their lives with, and the timid ones go on being shy with horses, or danger, or other people, or with themselves; their spirits, not their bodies, crippled. Mr. Sheehan said, England, the horse-growing country and the country as well of all the misfits, the hugger-muggers, the reticent, the mum, the evaders, because why, because what? because what except stuck up on a horse's back since generations and licked from the get-away, the lip set, both upper and lower, the eyes taught not to quail, and the heart broken in two by funk or daring at the age of five or younger. Take away the horses and you would have a fine upstanding race of men, the Britons, said Mr. Sheehan, the side of his face in profile squinted up either against laughing or against the drifting Irish weather, and for an instant she remembered the first time being thrown: the hack had cantered her up the lane to the top of the hill and there he had reared for no reason except "frightened by the bush because the bush unexpectedly turned and waved a branch," without warning dropping her the long way down. I remember being sick, terrifically sick, she thought, perhaps passing Apby at the thirty-foot

173

mark now, and mother made me mount quickly again as soon as I was finished being sick. "If you don't mount right away," mother said, "you'll start crying and then you won't want to get up on a horse again," and now Apby's voice called out, "One, two, three," and she put her teeth together and thought in sudden wild jubilation, Tomorrow I'll be able to tell Mr. Sheehan that at thirty feet from the fence I increased the stride to seven feet, then to eight, and finally to nine, at this point being, as near as I could judge in the dark, six feet from the jump and I gave my horse the office from the leap.

"Bat," she said quickly. "I can't see any more than you can but we're going to take it." She let the head free then and the loins free, and her weight moved swiftly into the knees as they clasped the saddle-flaps. The balls of the feet were riding lightly in the stirrup irons now and she held him firmly to the fence with her legs. At once she felt him rising strongly but sweetly under her, the mouth limber, the neck pliant even though stretched to go, no sense of heat or excitement confusing him but the blood as temperate as if he still cantered easily across the paddock. Just as they cleared what, from conjecture, must have been the rail though lost and undelineated in the night's and the falling water's obscurity, she thought of the other side and the wet grass where he might bog or slip at the landing, and she said again: "Damn it, oh, damn the rain."

She leaned with him, the body that had followed through the rise and the soaring now bending with him through the descent, and as his forefeet struck the ground her knees and ankles caught the shock and broke it but her hands did not move on the reins. She let him stride on for twenty yards or more before she pulled him up and turned him on his hocks, and halted there in the rain and darkness and listening to the coming and going of his breath, she called out to the groom:

"Apby, I say, Apby, come and open the gate for us," her own voice sounding ringing and clear. "Apby!" she called, like someone tipsy with triumph, drunk and reeling with it. "Apby, hurry up! I want to take him over again."

HORSE

Jim Harrison

A
quarter horse, no rider
canters through the pasture

thistles raise soft purple burrs
her flanks are shiny in the sun

I whistle and she runs
almost sideways toward me

the oats in my hand are sweets to her:

dun mane furling in its breeze,
her neck
corseted with muscle,
wet teeth friendly against my hand—
how can I believe
you ran under a low maple limb
to knock me off?

ALL IN GREEN WENT MY LOVE RIDING

E. E. Cummings

All in green went my love riding
on a great horse of gold
into the silver dawn.

four lean hounds crouched low and smiling
the merry deer ran before.

Fleeter be they than dappled dreams
the swift sweet deer
the red rare deer.

Four red roebuck at a white water
the cruel bugle sang before.

Horn at hip went my love riding
riding the echo down
into the silver dawn.

four lean hounds crouched low and smiling
the level meadows ran before.

Softer be they than slippered sleep
the lean lithe deer
the fleet flown deer.

Four fleet does at a gold valley
the famished arrow sang before.

Bow at belt went my love riding
riding the mountain down
into the silver dawn.

four lean hounds crouched low and smiling
the sheer peaks ran before.

Paler be they than daunting death
the sleek slim deer
the tall tense deer.

Four tall stags at a green mountain
the lucky hunter sang before.

All in green went my love riding
on a great horse of gold
into the silver dawn.

four lean hounds crouched low and smiling
my heart fell dead before.

From: ALL CREATURES GREAT AND SMALL

James Herriot

The two horses turned towards us at the sound. They were standing fetlock deep in the pebbly shallows just beyond a little beach which merged into the green carpet of turf; nose to tail, they had been rubbing their chins gently along each other's backs, unconscious of our approach. A high cliff overhanging the far bank made a perfect wind break while on either side of us clumps of oak and beech blazed in the autumn sunshine.

'They're in a nice spot, Mr. Skipton,' I said.

'Aye, they can keep cool in the hot weather and they've got the barn when winter comes.' John pointed to a low, thick-walled building with a single door. 'They can come and go as they please.'

The sound of his voice brought the horses out of the river at a stiff trot and as they came near you could see they really were old. The mare was a chestnut and the gelding was a light bay but their coats were so flecked with grey that they almost looked like roans. This was most pronounced on their faces where the sprinkling of white hairs, the sunken eyes and the deep cavity above the eyes gave them a truly venerable appearance.

For all that, they capered around John with a fair attempt at skittishness, stamping their feet, throwing their heads about, pushing his cap over his eyes with their muzzles.

'Get by, leave off!' he shouted. 'Daft awd beggars.' But he tugged absently at the mare's forelock and ran his hand briefly along the neck of the gelding.

'When did they last do any work?' I asked.

'Oh, about twelve years ago, I reckon.'

I stared at John. 'Twelve years! And have they been down here all that time?'

'Aye, just lakin' about down here, retired like. They've earned it an' all.' For a few moments he stood silent, shoulders hunched, hands deep in the pockets of his coat, then he spoke quietly as if to himself. 'They were two slaves when I was a slave.' He turned and looked at me

and for a revealing moment I read in the pale blue eyes something of the agony and struggle he had shared with the animals.

'But twelve years! How old are they, anyway?'

John's mouth twisted up at one corner. 'Well you're t'vet. You tell me.'

I stepped forward confidently, my mind buzzing with Galvayne's groove, shape of marks, degree of slope and the rest; I grasped the unprotesting upper lip of the mare and looked at her teeth.

'Good God!' I gasped, 'I've never seen anything like this.' The incisors were immensely long and projecting forward till they met at an angle of about forty-five degrees. There were no marks at all—they had long since gone.

I laughed and turned back to the old man. 'It's no good, I'd only be guessing. You'll have to tell me.'

'Well she's about thirty and gelding's a year or two younger. She's had fifteen grand foals and never ailed owt except a bit of teeth trouble. We've had them rasped a time or two and it's time they were done again, I reckon. They're both losing ground and dropping bits of half chewed hay from their mouths. Gelding's the worst—has a right job champin' his grub.'

I put my hand into the mare's mouth, grasped her tongue and pulled it out to one side. A quick exploration of the molars with my other hand revealed what I suspected; the outside edges of the upper teeth were overgrown and jagged and were irritating the cheeks while the inside edges of the lower molars were in a similar state and were slightly excoriating the tongue.

'I'll soon make her more comfortable, Mr. Skipton. With those sharp edges rubbed off she'll be as good as new.' I got the rasp out of my vast box, held the tongue in one hand and worked the rough surface along the teeth, checking occasionally with my fingers till the points had been sufficiently reduced.

'That's about right,' I said after a few minutes. 'I don't want to make them too smooth or she won't be able to grind her food.'

John grunted. 'Good enough. Now have a look at t'other. There's summat far wrong with him.'

I had a feel at the gelding's teeth. 'Just the same as the mare. Soon put him right, too.'

But pushing at the rasp, I had an uncomfortable feeling that something was not quite right. The thing wouldn't go fully to the back of the mouth; something was stopping it. I stopped rasping and explored again, reaching with my fingers as far as I could. And I came upon something very strange, something which shouldn't have been there at all. It was like a great chunk of bone projecting down from the roof of the mouth.

It was time I had a proper look. I got out my pocket torch and shone it over the back of the tongue. It was easy to see the trouble now; the last upper molar was overlapping the lower one resulting in a gross overgrowth of the posterior border. The result was a sabre-like barb about three inches long stabbing down into the tender tissue of the gum.

That would have to come off—right now. My jauntiness vanished and I suppressed a shudder; it meant using the horrible shears—those great long-handled things with the screw operated by a cross bar. They gave me the willies because I am one of those people who can't bear to watch anybody blowing up a balloon and this was the same sort of thing only worse. You fastened the sharp blades of the shears on to the tooth and began to turn the bar slowly, slowly. Soon the tooth began to groan and creak under the tremendous leverage and you knew that any second it would break off and when it did it was like somebody letting off a rifle in your ear. That was when all hell usually broke loose but mercifully this was a quiet old horse and I wouldn't expect him to start dancing around on his hind legs. There was no pain for the horse because the overgrown part had no nerve supply—it was the noise that caused the trouble.

Returning to my crate I produced the dreadful instrument and with it a Haussman's gag which I inserted on the incisors and opened on its ratchet till the mouth gaped wide. Everything was easy to see then and, of course, there it was—a great prong at the other side of the mouth exactly like the first. Great, great, now I had two to chop off.

The old horse stood patiently, eyes almost closed, as though he had seen it all and nothing in the world was going to bother him. I went through the motions with my toes curling and when the sharp crack came, the white-bordered eyes opened wide, but only in mild surprise. He never even moved. When I did the other side he paid no attention at all; in fact, with the gag prising his jaws apart he looked exactly as though he was yawning with boredom.

As I bundled the tools away, John picked up the bony spicules from the grass and studied them with interest. 'Well, poor awd beggar. Good job I got you along, young man. Reckon he'll feel a lot better now.'

On the way back, old John, relieved of his bale, was able to go twice as fast and he stumped his way up the hill at a furious pace, using the fork as a staff. I panted along in the rear, changing the box from hand to hand every few minutes.

About halfway up, the thing slipped out of my grasp and it gave me a chance to stop for a breather. As the old man muttered impatiently I looked back and could just see the two horses; they had

returned to the shallows and were playing together, chasing each other jerkily, their feet splashing in the water. The cliff made a dark backcloth to the picture—the shining river, the trees glowing bronze and gold and the sweet green of the grass.

Back in the farm yard, John paused awkwardly. He nodded once or twice, said 'Thank ye, young man,' then turned abruptly and walked away.

I was dumping the box thankfully into the boot when I saw the man who had spoken to us on the way down. He was sitting, cheerful as ever, in a sunny corner, back against a pile of sacks, pulling his dinner packet from an old army satchel.

'You've been down to see t'pensioners then? By gaw, awd John should know the way.'

'Regular visitor, is he?'

'Regular? Every day God sends you'll see t'awd feller ploddin' down there. Rain, snow or blow, never misses. And allus has summat with him—bag o' corn, straw for their bedding.'

'And he's done that for twelve years?'

The man unscrewed his thermos flask and poured himself a cup of black tea. 'Aye, them 'osses haven't done a stroke o' work all that time and he could've got good money for them from the horse flesh merchants. Rum 'un, isn't it?'

'You're right,' I said, 'it is a rum 'un.'

Just how rum it was occupied my thoughts on the way back to the surgery. I went back to my conversation with Siegfried that morning; we had just about decided that the man with a lot of animals couldn't be expected to feel affection for individuals among them. But those buildings back there were full of John Skipton's animals—he must have hundreds.

Yet what made him trail down that hillside every day in all weathers? Why had he filled the last years of those two old horses with peace and beauty? Why had he given them a final ease and comfort which he had withheld from himself?

It could only be love.

HORSES AND COWBOYS
TO BE HORSEBACK

Drummond Hadley

Sitting on top of a dun horse,
Feeling his legs running underneath you,
Feeling all that he is at the touch of a rein,
Ready to whirl or set up on a dime,
Ready to carry us across blue mountain ranges,
Ready to cross *barrancas* and arroyos,
Ready to fly when we take down our rope
To catch any wild heifer
Who breaks to run when we want her,
Ready to stop, to stay, still listening,
For whatever it is we're waiting to hear,
Feeling the beat of that pounding breath,
Hooves and heart whirling under you,
That's what it's like to be horseback.
That's what it's like to be a cowboy.

From: BLACK BEAUTY

Anna Sewell

One day during this summer, the groom cleaned and dressed me with such extraordinary care, that I thought some new change must be at hand; he trimmed my fetlocks and legs, passed the tarbrush over my hoofs, and even parted my forelock. I think the harness had an extra polish. Willie seemed half anxious, half merry, as he got into the chaise with his grandfather.

'If the ladies take to him,' said the old gentleman, 'they'll be suited, and he'll be suited: we can but try.'

At the distance of a mile or two from the village, we came to a pretty, low house, with a lawn and shrubbery at the front and a drive up to the door. Willie rang the bell, and asked if Miss Blomefield or Miss Ellen was at home. Yes, they were. So, whilst Willie stayed with me, Mr. Thoroughbood went into the house. In about ten minutes he returned, followed by three ladies; one tall, pale lady, wrapped in a white shawl, leaned on a younger, with dark eyes and a merry face; the other, a very stately-looking person, was Miss Blomefield. They all came and looked at me and asked questions. The younger lady—that was Miss Ellen— took to me very much; she said she was sure she should like me, I had such a good face. The tall, pale lady said that she should always be nervous in riding behind a horse that had once been down, as I might come down again, and if I did, she should never get over the fright.

'You see, ladies,' said Mr. Thoroughgood, 'many first-rate horses have had their knees broken through the carelessness of their drivers, without any fault of their own, and from what I see of this horse, I should say that is his case; but of course I do not wish to influence you. If you incline, you can have him on trial, and then your coachman will see what he thinks of him.'

'You have always been such a good adviser to us about our horses,' said the stately lady, 'that your recommendation would go a long way with me, and if my sister Lavinia sees no objection, we will accept your offer of a trial, with thanks.'

It was then arranged that I should be sent for the next day.

In the morning a smart-looking young man came for me. At first, he looked pleased, but when he saw my knees, he said in a disappointed voice:

'I didn't think, sir, you would have recommended my ladies a blemished horse like that.'

' "Handsome is—that handsome does," ' said my master, 'you are only taking him on trial, and I am sure you will do fairly by him, young man, and if he is not as safe as any horse you ever drove, send him back.'

I was led home, placed in a comfortable stable, fed, and left to myself. The next day, when my groom was cleaning my face, he said:

'That is just like the star that Black Beauty had, he is much the same height too. I wonder where he is now.'

A little farther on, he came to the place in my neck where I was bled, and where a little knot was left in the skin. He almost started, and began to look me over carefully, talking to himself.

'White star in the forehead, one white foot on the off side, this little knot just in that place.' Then, looking at the middle of my back— 'and as I am alive, there is that little patch of white hair that John used to call "Beauty's threepenny bit". It *must* be Black Beauty! Why, Beauty! Beauty! Do you know me? Little Joe Green, that almost killed you?' And he began patting and patting me as if he was quite overjoyed.

I could not say that I remembered him, for now he was a fine grown young fellow, with black whiskers and a man's voice, but I was sure he knew me, and that he was Joe Green, and I was very glad. I put my nose up to him, and tried to say we were friends. I never saw a man so pleased.

'Give you a fair trial! I should think so indeed! I wonder who the rascal was that broke your knees, my old Beauty! You must have been badly served out somewhere. Well, well, it won't be my fault if you haven't good times of it now. I wish John Manly was here to see you.'

In the afternoon I was put into a low Park chair and brought to the door. Miss Ellen was going to try me, and Green went with her. I soon found that she was a good driver, and she seemed pleased with my paces. I heard Joe telling her about me, and that he was sure I was Squire Gordon's old Black Beauty.

When we returned, the other sisters came out to hear how I had behaved myself. She told them what she had just heard, and said:

'I shall certainly write to Mrs. Gordon, and tell her that her favourite horse has come to us. How pleased she will be!"

After this I was driven every day for a week or so, and as I appeared to be quite safe, Miss Lavinia at last ventured out in the small close carriage. After this it was quite decided to keep me and call me by my old name of 'Black Beauty'.

I have now lived in this happy place a whole year. Joe is the best and kindest of grooms. My work is easy and pleasant, and I feel my strength and spirits all coming back again. Mr. Thoroughgood said to Joe the other day:

'In your place he will last till he is twenty years old—perhaps more.'

Willie always speaks to me when he can, and treats me as his special friend. My ladies have promised that I shall never be sold, and so I have nothing to fear; and here my story ends. My troubles are all over, and I am at home; and often before I am quite awake, I fancy I am still in the orchard at Birtwick, standing with my old friends under the apple trees.

LAURA CHESTER has been writing, editing, and publishing poetry, fiction, and non-fiction since the early seventies. Editor of the first 20th Century American Women Poets anthology, *Rising Tides*, she went on to edit several important collections, including *Deep Down* (Faber & Faber), and *The Unmade Bed* (HarperCollins). Her most recent books include a new edition of *Lupus Novice* (Station Hill Press), a short story collection, *Bitches Ride Alone* (Black Sparrow Press), the novels *The Story of the Lake* (Faber & Faber) and *Kingdom Come* (Creative Arts Book Company). Indiana University Press published the non-fiction book, *Holy Personal*, with photographs by Donna DeMari. Chester lives in Patagonia, Arizona, as well as the Berkshires of Massachusetts. Her most recent book, *Hiding Glory*, will be published by Willow Creek Press in the fall of 2007. www.laurachester.com

DONNA DEMARI has been shooting fashion and fine arts photography since the late seventies. Her work has appeared in many top European magazines, including *Vogue, Elle,* and *Marie Claire.* A show of her horse photographs, "Flying Mane," was held at the SAS Gallery. Her photographs were included in the book of selected prose-poems, *Sparks*, by Laura Chester. DeMari was also the photographer for *Holy Personal*, published by Indiana University Press. www.donnademari.com.

ACKNOWLEDGEMENTS

Grateful acknowledgment is made to the authors and publishers for use of the following material. While every effort has been made to obtain permission, there may still be cases in which we have failed to trace a copyright holder, and we would like to apologize for any apparent negligence. If notified, the publisher will be pleased to rectify an omission in future editions.

Bagnold, Enid. From: *National Velvet*, copyright © 1935 by Enid Bagnold. William Morrow publisher. Reprinted by permission of the estate of Enid Bagnold.

Boyle, Kay. Excerpt from "The Crazy Hunter," from *Three Short Novels*, copyright © 1940 by Kay Boyle. Reprinted by permission of New Directions Publishing Corp.

Brown, Nancy Marie. From *A Good Horse Has No Color*, copyright © Nancy Marie Brown. Reprinted by permission of Stackpole Books.

Chester, Laura. Excerpt from *Free Rein*, copyright © 1988 by Laura Chester. Reprinted with permission of Burning Deck Press.

Chester, Laura. Excerpt from *The Story of the Lake*, copyright © 1995 by Laura Chester, Faber & Faber. Reprinted by permission of the author.

Cummings, E.E. "All in green went my love riding". Copyright 1923, 1951, © 1991 by the Trustees for the E.E. Cummings Trust. Copyright © 1976 by George James Firmage, from *Complete Poems: 1904-1962* by E.E. Cummings, edited by George J. Firmage. Used by permission of Liveright Publishing Corporation.

Edson, Russell. "The Horse of Fashion," copyright © Russell Edson. Reprinted by permission of the author.

Francis, Dick. Excerpt from *The Sport of Queens*, copyright © by Dick Francis. Reprinted by permission of SLL/Sterling Lord Literistic, Inc.

Fuller, Alexandra. From *Don't Let's Go to the Dogs Tonight* by Alexandra Fuller, copyright © 2001 by Alexandra Fuller. Used by permission of Random House, Inc.

Gerber, Dan. "The View from the Pasture," copyright © Dan Gerber. Reprinted by permission of the author.

Giono, Jean. From *Joy of Man's Desiring*, copyright © 1980 by Aline Giono. Reprinted by permission of Counterpoint, a member of Perseus Books, LLC.

Grealy, Lucy. Excerpt from *Autobiography of a Face* by Lucy Grealy. Copyright © 1994 by Lucy Grealy. Reprinted by permission of Houghton Mifflin Company. All rights reserved.

Grealy, Lucy. "A Brief Sketch of Myself at Fourteen," from *As Seen On TV: Provocations*, copyright © Lucy Grealy. Reprinted by permission of Bloomsbury, USA.

Gruen, Sara. From *Riding Lessons*, copyright © 2004 by Sara Gruen. Reprinted by permission of HarperCollins Publishers.

Hadley, Drummond. "Horses and Cowboys, To Be Horseback," from *Voice of the Borderlands*, copyright © 2005 by Drummond Hadley. Reprinted by permission of Rio Nuevo Publishers.

Harrison, Jim. "Horse" from *The Shape of the Journey: New and Collected Poems*, copyright © 1998 by Jim Harrison. Published by Copper Canyon Press. Reprinted by permission of the author. All rights reserved.

Hawkes, John. From *Sweet William: The Memoirs of Old Horse* by John Hawkes. Copyright © 1993 by John Hawkes. Reprinted with permission of Simon & Schuster Adult Publishing Group.

Heaney, Seamus. "The Forge" from *Opened Ground: Selected Poems 1966-1996* by Seamus Heaney. Copyright © 1998 by Seamus Heaney. Reprinted by permission of Farrar, Straus and Giroux, LLC, and Faber & Faber Ltd.

Henry, Marguerite. From *King of the Wind* by Marguerite Henry. Text copyright 1948 and copyright renewed © 1976 by Marguerite Henry. Reprinted with the permission of Simon & Schuster Books for Young Readers, an imprint of Simon & Schuster Children's Publishing Division.

Henry, Marguerite. From *Misty of Chincoteague* by Marguerite Henry. Text copyright 1947 and renewed © 1975 by Marguerite Henry. Reprinted with the permission of Simon & Schuster Books for Young Readers, an imprint of Simon & Schuster Children's Publishing Division.

Herriot, James. From "It Shouldn't Happen to a Vet," from *All Creatures Great and Small*, copyright © 1972 by James Herriot. Reprinted by permission of Harold Ober Associates Incorporated and St. Martin's Press, LLC.

Hughes, Ted. "The Horses" from *Collected Poems* by Ted Hughes. Copyright © 2003 by The Estate of Ted Hughes. Reprinted by permission of Farrar, Straus and Giroux, LLC, and Faber & Faber Ltd.

Koncel, Mary. "Song," from *You Can Tell the Horse Anything*, copyright © 2003 by Mary Koncel. All rights reserved. Reprinted by permission of Tupelo Press.

Korda, Michael. Excerpt from *Horse People*, copyright © 2003 by Success Research Corporation. Reprinted by permission of HarperCollins Publishers.

Kumin, Maxine. "Amanda is Shod", from *Selected Poems 1960-1990* by Maxine Kumin. Copyright © 1996 by Maxine Kumin. Used by permission of W.W. Norton & Company, Inc.

Kumin, Maxine. "Praise Be", from *Looking for Luck* by Maxine Kumin. Copyright © 1992 by Maxine Kumin. Used by permission of W.W. Norton & Company, Inc.

Lawrence, D.H. Excerpt from *St. Mawr and The Man Who Died* by D.H. Lawrence, copyright © 1928 by Alfred A. Knopf, Inc. Used by permission of Alfred A. Knopf, a division of Random House, Inc.

Lifshin, Lyn. Excerpts from *The Licorice Daughter: My Year with Ruffian*, copyright © 2005 by Lyn Lifshin, Texas Review Press. Reprinted by permission of the author and publisher.

Mitchell, Elyne. Excerpt from *The Silver Brumby*, copyright © 1958, first published by E.P. Dutton & Co., Inc. Reprinted by permission of Curtis Brown AU, and the estate of Elyne Mitchell.

Petroski, Catherine. From "Beautiful My Mane in the Wind," copyright © Catherine Petroski. Used by permission of the author; first published in *North American Review*, Fall 1975.

Podhajsky, Alois. Excerpt from *My Horses My Teachers*, by Col. Alois Podhajsky. Originally published by Doubleday & Company, 1968; republished by Trafalgar Square Publishing, N. Pomfret, VT. Used by permission of Trafalgar Square Publishing.

Seredy, Kate. From *The Good Master* by Kate Seredy, copyright 1935 by Kate Seredy, renewed © 1963 by Kate Seredy. Used by permission of Viking Penguin, A Division of Penguin Young Readers Group, A Member of Penguin Group (USA) Inc., 345 Hudson Street, New York, NY 10014. All rights reserved.

Smiley, Jane. Excerpt from Chapter nine from *Barn Blind* by Jane Smiley. Copyright © 1980 by Jane Graves Smiley. Reprinted by permission of HarperCollins Publishers.

Spragg, Mark. Excerpt from *Where Rivers Change Direction*, copyright © 1999 by Mark Spragg. Reprinted by permission of the author. All rights reserved.

Yoors, Yan. Excerpt from *The Gypsies*, copyright 1967, reissued © 1987. Reprinted by permission of Waveland Press, Inc., Long Grove, IL. All rights reserved.

Zarzyski, Paul. "She Holds Her Favorite Cowboy Close," from *All This Way for the Short Ride, Poems*, copyright © 1996 by Paul Zarsyski. Published by the Museum of New Mexico Press. Reprinted by permission of the author. All rights reserved.